MW01105732

The Perfect Norm

How to Teach Differentially, Assess Effectively, and Manage a Classroom Ethically in Ways That Are "Brain-Friendly" and Culturally Responsive

A volume in
Literacy, Language, and Learning
Patricia Ruggiano Schmidt, *Series Editor*

The Perfect Norm

How to Teach Differentially, Assess Effectively, and Manage a Classroom Ethically in Ways That Are "Brain-Friendly" and Culturally Responsive

Sharon L. Spencer
North Carolina Central University

Sandra A. Vavra
North Carolina Central University

Foreword by
Patricia Ruggiano Schmidt

INFORMATION AGE PUBLISHING, INC.
Charlotte, NC • www.infoagepub.com

Library of Congress Cataloging-in-Publication Data

Spencer, Sharon L.
  The perfect norm : how to teach differentially, assess effectively, and
manage a classroom ethically in ways that are "brain-friendly" and
culturally responsive / Sharon L. Spencer, Sandra A. Vavra.
      p. cm.
  Includes bibliographical references.
  ISBN 978-1-60752-033-7 (pbk.) – ISBN 978-1-60752-034-4 (hardcover)
  1. Effective teaching. 2. Classroom management. 3. Cultural awareness.
I. Vavra, Sandra. II. Title.
  LB1025.3.S65 2009
  371.102–dc22

                                                    2008051150

Printed in the United States of America

CONTENTS

Acknowledgements vii

Foreword ix
    Patricia Ruggiano Schmidt

Preface xv

1 A Case for Differentiation and Much More 1

2 The Fabric of My Life: Using Poetry, Prose, and Graphic
    Novels to Help Students Reflect Upon Their Identities 25

3 Choices That Change Our Lives: Using Realistic Fiction and
    Nonfiction to Help Students Reflect on Difficult Decisions 45

4 Community and Culture: Understanding Ourselves and
    Others in the Global Community 71

5 A Journey from Innocence to Experience: A Course in Young
    Adult Literature for Future Teachers... 97

6 Convince Me: A Syllabus for a Freshman Composition Course
    Focused on Writing Arguments 117

About the Authors 143

Index.. 145

ACKNOWLEDGEMENTS

To Caryl, who so generously shared with me her knowledge about how to teach and nurture intelligent, caring, principled, happy human beings— and to my daughter Jessica, who is one.

—Sandy

To Sandy, who nudged me into *really* doing this project; Pat, who helped me realize my dream to become a teacher; Cecelia and Pauletta, who have consistently shown faith in me; to my mother, brothers, and sister, who have always been there; and to my family—Charlie, Spencer, and Emma—who always support me in my work and love me despite of it.

—Sharon

FOREWORD

Patricia Ruggiano Schmidt

When we listen to successful teachers, we often hear concepts, such as "drawing upon student prior knowledge to establish understandings of content," "connecting the known to the new for motivating and creating meaningful student learning," "presenting 'brain-friendly' strategies for student active involvement and inquiry," and "connecting home, school, and community for culturally responsive pedagogy." All of these concepts are based on knowing students as individuals in order to better facilitate teaching and learning. And these concepts directly relate to Critical Literacy (Nebeker,1998; Shor, 1992).

Unfortunately, we don't see enough teachers practicing these ideas. But, fortunately, *The Perfect Norm: How to Teach Differentially, Assess Effectively, and Manage a Classroom Ethically in Ways That Are "Brain-friendly" and Culturally Responsive*, by Sharon L. Spencer and Sandra A. Vavra is a text that assists secondary educators, as well as higher education instructors, in developing critical literacy in their classrooms and schools.

WHAT IS CRITICAL LITERACY?

Critical literacy is rooted in the work of critical theorists who believe that there are groups in society who see themselves as the mainstream power brokers (Friere, 1970; Moll, Amanti, Neff, & Gonzalez, 1992; Nieto, 1996;

The Perfect Norm, pages ix–xiii
Copyright © 2009 by Information Age Publishing
All rights of reproduction in any form reserved.

Ladson-billings, 1999; Sleeter, 2001). These privileged people have carved out financial, educational, and social security, with the aid of a strong sociopolitical system . . . a system structured in ways that discriminate against linguistic, economic, ethnic, and cultural differences. Consequently, educational theorists who embrace critical literacy see our school systems as places where this oppressive social structure is propagated.

Critical literacy theorists (Bernal, 2002; Duncan, 2002; Fernandez, 2002; Solorzano & Yosso, 2002) propose that we listen to the stories of the oppressed in our society, so that we might achieve a better understanding of problematic social structures. Additionally, they suggest that qualitative research methodologies provide the best venues for recording and reporting the voices of the oppressed. Moreover, critical literacy theorists exhort researchers to not only write, but also to speak and organize action for change. They see a great need for more equitable and democratic systems and structures.

Therefore, in sync with *The Perfect Norm: How to Teach Differentially, Assess Effectively, and Manage a Classroom Ethically in Ways That Are "Brain-friendly" and Culturally Responsive* and critical literacy theorists, I challenge readers and authors to promote critical literacy theory more explicitly. I will add examples for each chapter of this book, examples that amplify the voices of students, families, and community members. Finally, I will end with three invitations that would begin to change school structures and promote a more democratic system for our nation.

MORE EXAMPLES OF CRITICAL LITERACY

Chapter 1 is a thorough and brilliantly organized rationale for this book, giving readers the theoretical framework for attempting units that directly relate to critical literacy. I would challenge the readers to add to this framework by systematically collecting classroom data to prove that these are practical ideas for listening to students' voices and improving student achievement. Such proof could propel schools to adopt more democratic principles.

Chapter 2 is a wonderful opportunity to make learning relevant through student autobiographies. It is a superior way to develop a productive learning community. Students may also wish to interview each other to discover similarities and differences, thus setting the stage for an appreciation of human differences. Of course, before attempting this, appropriate interview techniques need to be modeled. I would also challenge teachers to write their own autobiographies first, so that they may better understand the student assignment. Portions of teachers' and students' lives could be shared, thus promoting equity in the teaching and learning community, another principle of critical literacy.

Chapter 3 is the perfect example of making learning real. Helping students deal with life decisions in rational and positive ways sets the stage for happy and productive years ahead. "Bibliotherapy" was a term used in the 1960s by literacy professors to describe literature that met individual interests and needs of students. The claim was made that if a student were matched to an appropriate piece of literature, he or she would become a lifelong reader. This chapter's challenge is to include authentic student problems, implement problem-solving techniques, and follow-up on results. Personal testimonies could be powerful. Authentic student voices would be heard in the classroom, again promoting critical literacy.

Chapter 4 stresses the need to understand and appreciate diversity at the local, national, and global levels. The fantastic activities in this chapter inspire! The challenge here is to invite visitors who represent linguistic, ethnic, economic, and cultural diversity to be interviewed by the class. The visitors might present a story, a powerpoint presentation, and/or artifacts from their backgrounds. Additionally, the class could visit diverse sites in the community, such as a First Nation People's school, a mosque, a temple, or a specific group's cultural activity. (I also escort my classes to Samrhat, a restaurant owned by people from Northern India.) Introducing students to other languages and cultures awakens interests in differing human perspectives, thus inspiring inquiry. This inquiry stimulates thinking about similarities and differences and how an understanding of diverse perspectives is essential to global survival, a basic tenet of critical literacy.

Chapter 5 teaches the value of the various genres of literature. Its methods and materials are useful and will develop the knowledge required for "brain-friendly" activities. For this chapter, I would challenge teachers and students to dramatize literature. This is a time-consuming suggestion, but one that allows the teacher and students to see each other in very different ways. Sometimes, the quietest student is the biggest "ham." Dramatic presentations promote self-confidence and create many opportunities for collegial humor. Students become stars, directors, scene designers, costume and make-up specialists, and musical producers. This kind of participatory learning and teaching is unforgettable and is based, again, on creating democratic learning environments.

Chapter 6 deals with the basics of writing in Standard English. I have always encouraged my students to write in their "love languages" as well as standard English, giving credence to the bilingual nature of our communication. For example, I write a note to a friend about my vacation in Alaska, I write a note to my grandson about my vacation in Alaska, I write a note to the travel agent who helped me plan my vacation in Alaska, and I write a note to the governor of Alaska about my vacation. The notes vary in content and formalities . . . I may not even consider punctuation when writing to a friend, but I would be very careful when writing to the governor. So my point is . . . audience matters. By explaining to students that audience is a consideration when writing, students see communication as a complex process that seeks to make meaning. This helps students gain confidence in their writing, but also promotes an understanding of the importance of proper communication. Thoughtful communication inspires and critical literacy sees it as essential to gaining access to all groups of people. I also challenge the readers and authors to invite amateur and professional writers to visit the classroom to learn what Hemingway said so well, "it's easy to write . . . just sit at your typewriter and bleed." There is no doubt that writing is difficult for everyone.

These additional specific challenges for each chapter contribute to starting small . . . baby steps toward critical literacy where classrooms become learning communities for teachers and students. And to paraphrase Friere (1970), "Critical literacy learning occurs when students and teachers dialogue both in and out of the classroom . . . where teachers and students share their lives for teaching and learning, thus empowering all involved."

To summarize this final word regarding *The Perfect Norm: How to Teach Differentially, Assess Effectively, and Manage a Classroom Ethically in Ways That Are "Brain-friendly" and Culturally Responsive*, I invite readers and authors to think beyond the book's unique units of study and accomplish the following:

- Adapt and implement these expertly organized ideas and begin action research in their own classrooms and schools.
- Collect and analyze qualitative and quantitative data from classroom implementation.
- Disseminate the action research and the qualitative and quantitative research in journals, books, and in-service and pre-service programs.

The process of accomplishing these tasks as well as the results will begin to structurally change our educational system. As the authors of this book and those who implement and adapt the ideas and strategies in this book go forth and make changes in their classrooms and schools, they will be developing a truly democratic society that values similar and different perspectives for enriched national and international communication.

REFERENCES

Bernal, D. (2002). Critical race theory, Latino critical theory, and critical raced-gendered epistemologies: Recognizing students of color as holders and creators of knowledge. *Qualitative Inquiry, 8*, 105–126.

Duncan,G. (2002). Critical race theory and method: Rendering race in urban ethnographic research. *Qualitative Inquiry, 8*, 85–104.

Fernandez, L. (2002). Telling stories about school: Using critical race theories to document Latina/Latino education and resistance. *Quantitative Inquiry, 8*, 45–65.

Friere, P. (1970). *Pedagogy of the oppressed.* New York: Continuum.

Ladson-billings, G. (1999). Preparing teachers for diverse student populations: A critical race theory perspective. In A. Iran Nejad & P. D. Pearson (Eds.), *Review of research in education* (Vol. 24, pp. 211–247). Washington, DC: American Educational Research Association.

Moll, L. C., Amanti, C., Neff, D., & Gonzalez, N. (1992). Funds of knowledge for teaching: Using a qualitative approach to connect homes and classrooms. *Theory Into Practice, 31*, 132–141.

Nebeker, K. C. (1998). Critical race theory: A White graduate student's struggle with the growing area of scholarship. *International Journal of Qualitative Studies in Education, 11*, 25–41.

Nieto, S. (1996). *Affirming diversity: The sociopolitical context of multicultural education.* New York: Longman.

Shor, I. (1992). *Empowering education: Critical teaching for social change.* University of Chicago Press.

Sleeter, C. E. (2001). Preparing teachers for culturally diverse schools. *Journal of Teacher Education, 52*(2), 94–106.

Solorzano, D., & Yosso, T. (2002). Critical race methodology: Counter-storytelling as an analytical framework. *Qualitative Inquiry, 8*, 23–44.

PREFACE

Student success is the ultimate goal for teachers, administrators, parents, and other stakeholders. Although these groups have the same goal, they often find themselves at odds because of the political nature of schools and schooling. While *assessment* and *accountability* are really important, these two words have taken on a meaning all their own. They are like the monsters in the closet that keep us from sleeping at night. In some ways, our teachers *feel* they are being told two very different things. First, *students must pass the test!* Second, *teachers must meet the needs of all learners,* who are diverse along a multitude of dimensions. What we believe is that actively engaging all learners in a variety of learning opportunities that promote higher order thinking *will* lead to higher test scores. We do *not* believe that the current curriculum lends itself to lower order thinking, worksheets, lecture, and textbook learning.

Although there very well may be some monsters in the closet, we believe that this can be the "best of times," not the "worst of times." Why do we think it is the best of times? We believe that there are so many exciting approaches and strategies available to "grab" students, including the newest en vogue term: "brain-friendly." Although neuroscientists may cringe when educators talk about "brain-friendly" teaching because so much is yet unknown about the brain, the strategies themselves have educational merit. When teachers incorporate a variety of "brain-friendly" strategies, they are actively engaging students and, typically, providing practice in a variety of novel ways to reinforce learning. They are meeting the needs of those who must **see it, hear it,** or **feel it** through tactile or kinesthetic modes. When teachers give students a voice in and ownership of their learning, students become invested. Once invested, student achievement is inevitable. So, even if "brain-friendly" seems like a current educational buzzword, the result is a push to involve learners naturally and deeply in their own learning.

The Perfect Norm, pages xv–xvii
Copyright © 2009 by Information Age Publishing
All rights of reproduction in any form reserved.

Our goal in writing this book was to validate teachers for strong efforts in their life's work. We often observe teachers' frustrations with what they perceive to be a multitude of different hot topics in education that they must attend to now, but which they expect to come and go, like the last hot topics. So, we wanted to help readers see similarities between many of these hot topics—*differentiation, multiple intelligences, culturally responsive teaching, "brain-friendly" strategies, authentic assessment, and ethical classroom management*—which we feel are ***not*** flashes in the pan. And we trust that serious practitioners will not oversimplify the findings of neuroscientists and their application to education. Reading studies and books by scientists, a number of which are user-friendly, can help ensure that teachers separate the hype from credible information. We have seen this professionally judicious approach in the work of graduate students (Kolinski, 2007) in adopting "brain-friendly" strategies.

In Chapter 1, we develop "A Case for Differentiation and More" that argues our case. Then, in chapters two through six, we provide units as models for differentiating instruction at the middle, secondary, and university levels. We have observed that differentiation seems more difficult after elementary school because of the strong emphasis on content and testing, although some elementary teachers feel this struggle as well. We certainly know that it is difficult for university faculty who are, most often, teaching subjects. Nevertheless, the effort is well worth it. While teachers/faculty may not relish coming out of their comfort level as content-experts/lecturers, the tradeoff is that curriculum focuses more on essential knowledge and student engagement.

In Chapter 2, "The Fabric of My Life," students will explore their own identity and voice around four main questions: a) Who Am I?: The Voice Within; b) Where Do I Come From?: The Voice of the Past; c) How Do I Fit within the World?: The Voice of the Present; and d) What Are My Hopes and Aspirations?: The Voice of the Future. Students read ***and*** write poetry, stories, essays, and graphic novels.

In Chapter 3, "Choices That Change Our Lives," students reflect on difficult decisions that adolescents and young adults face. They read both fiction and nonfiction, engage in literature circles, work in teams, and teach each other.

In Chapter 4, "Community and Culture: Understanding Ourselves and Others in the Global Community," students learn about the historical, political, economic, and social community in which they live. This experience provides them with models for researching and developing comprehensive learning stations, so that they, in teams, can put together a comprehensive learning station about a country and then teach other teams who will be doing the same for a different country.

In Chapter 5, "A Journey from Innocence to Experience: A Course in Young Adult Literature for Future Teachers," middle and secondary teachers and university instructors are given a model for developing syllabi using a layered curriculum approach for a survey-type course. Within the layered curriculum, a variety of engaging activities and varied assessments are included.

In Chapter 6, "Convince Me—A Syllabus for a Freshman Composition Course Focused on Argumentative Writing," a model is provided, as in chapter five, for developing a syllabus comprising layered curriculum, a variety of engaging activities, and varied assessments. However, this syllabus is much more focused in its content and is process-oriented (since it is about writing) than the adolescent literature survey course.

HOW TO USE THIS BOOK

We have intentionally packed both theoretical/research-based and practical information in this book because professional educators want to know **why** they should use certain approaches, models, and strategies. In turn, as professionals, we should be able to explain why we teach the way we do– not to *justify*, but to *educate* others about our knowledge-based, reflective, decision-making processes and the impact on student learning. Thus, it is important to read Chapter 1 because it lays a foundation.

Each succeeding chapter (2–6) has unique and compelling twists and turns—chock full of ideas to use or to adapt. It is possible to gain lots of ideas, processes, and strategies from reading and implementing (or adapting) even one of the unit chapters, or a part of it. While some of the units are explicitly about literacy, others focus on content using reading, writing, speaking, and listening as critical in the learning process. Thus, literacy skills are reinforced and strengthened. Additionally, some of our colleagues and public school partners have given us feedback that *they* wanted to implement some of the units and activities *themselves*. So, feel free to use this book for self-exploration and professional development. We certainly did.

REFERENCE

Kolinski, M. (2007). *Perceptions of right brain and left brain learning.* Unpublished Master's thesis, LeMoyne College, Syracue, NY.

CHAPTER 1

A CASE FOR DIFFERENTIATION AND MUCH MORE...

When I think back on all the crap I learned in high school/
It's a wonder I can think at all.

—Paul Simon, *Kodachrome*

Teachers do not take a Hippocratic oath as they receive their licenses. Yet, whether they say it out loud or just keep it quietly to themselves as part of their worldview, they truly mean to "do no harm." If a survey were taken of teacher candidates in training, of idealistic beginning teachers, of seasoned master

---

teachers, and even of weary veterans on the verge of retirement, we believe all would check the "NO" column on each of the following statements:

NO YES
☐   ☐   I make it a habit to marginalize students.
☐   ☐   I like to design ways for struggling students to continually work at the frustration level.
☐   ☐   I respond to problem behaviors by meting out consequences according to race, gender, and socio-economic status.
☐   ☐   My grading practices compare students to each other and assume some students will fail and be left behind.
☐   ☐   I purposely create a dumbed-down curriculum to bore students into submission in my classroom or to drop out of school altogether.

The statements above seem ludicrous; yet, these beliefs *must be* being operationalized in classrooms across the country. If not, how do we explain these dismal observations of educational researchers?:

- African American males disproportionately receive consequences for behavior issues as compared to their White peers (Cartledge & Milburn, 1996).
- "American high school students have a poorer mastery of basic math concepts than their counterparts in most other leading industrialized nations....[Reasons why] range from the teacher shortage to a lack of sufficiently challenging math courses to an over-reliance on facile standardized tests" (Dobbs, 2004, pp.A1, A8).
- Many high-achieving learners remain unchallenged in their heterogeneous classrooms (Archambault et al., 1993).
- African-American males in the U.S., particularly those living in high poverty areas, are failing in our schools because they are not exposed to texts that are meaningful to their lives (Tatum, 2000, 2006).
- Student grades are often distorted, either by factors like neat handwriting or deflated by factors like slow work pace (Guskey & Bailey, 2001).
- "Labeling, teacher attitudes, and current practices marginalize students labeled as having dis/abilities" (Baglieri & Knopf, 2004, p. 526).
- Black students receive lengthier suspensions and at earlier ages, two to five times more than majority students (Irvine, 1990).

- Many grades lack clarity about what the grade actually represents (O'Connor, 2002).
- Only 23% of U.S. fourth-grade students and 31% of eighth-grade students scored at or above standard in writing (National Center for Research Statistics, 2002).
- "Forty-seven percent of the United States' nine-year-olds are reading disabled" (Nunley, 2003, p.23).
- "...the structure and practices of schools [e.g., rigid tracking, unevenly distributed resources, standardized testing] privilege select groups of students while marginalizing or segregating others" (Weinstein, Curran, Tomlinson-Clarke, 2003, p. 271).
- Normative grading practices spawn unhealthy competition and diminish student motivation (Wiggins, 1993).
- "...what we frequently do is ask students who have a disability in one region [of the brain] to just keep practicing that disabled skill, over and over and over" (Nunley, 2003, p. 106).

Unfortunately, as we search for the answers to why and how we arrived at this deplorable state of affairs, chief among the usual suspects to blame is the ironically named No Child Left Behind Act of 2001 (NCLB). Jay Mc-Tighe, an educational consultant for the Association for Supervision and Curriculum Development and member of the national training cadres for *Understanding by Design* and *What Works in Schools*, aptly expresses what many researchers and teacher practitioners have found: Efforts (whether they be by individual educators, schools, districts, or states) to achieve targets for continuous improvement have created a pedagogy highly mismatched with the needs of students. In a recent article (2005), McTighe and Brown cite four common educational practices which are counterproductive to promoting student engagement, literacy, and sustained achievement:

1. Excessively broad or overloaded written curricula that fail to articulate what is core or essential for deep understanding among all learners;
2. Educators' perceptions that they must cover every mandated standard within this "mile-wide, inch-deep" curriculum, in case it appears on a high-stakes accountability test;
3. One-size-fits-all worksheet-based teaching activities that model test questions and familiarize students with testing formats, frequently interrupting the true process of learning; and
4. Adoption of a reductionist, "teaching to the test" approach to boost scores on standardized assessments. (p. 235)

Bejoian and Reid (2005) are critical of NCLB, citing it as "dangerous in its focus on accountability testing, [serving] to further segregate the already marginalized students with LD and English language learners (p. 528). Wink (2000) adds that the "research-based" instructional programs and methods which No Child Left Behind favors discourages teachers from employing engaging teaching practices focused on students' interests and learning style preferences. It seems that while NCLB claims to support highly qualified teachers in their efforts to help all students achieve at high levels, the process it sets up is, in almost every way possible, antithetical to practices which promote real engagement and learning. Just under the surface of the encouraging words "no child left behind" is a very strong message of fear—aimed directly at teachers and schools which, in turn, pass the fear down to the students (in a variety of forms from general test anxiety to stress over scores not being high enough for acceptance at a favored college).

In "NCLB Fitfully Fits Differentiated Instruction," VanSciver (2005) ex-plicitly points out what teachers learned so well soon after the legislation went into effect: "Teachers and administrators are threatened with the public humiliation of negative labels if they cannot get students to 'make the grade'" (p. 37). A case in point is Betsy Talbott, a middle grades history teacher, who "abandoned" what she knew to be best teaching practices after receiving continuous pressure from school and district administra-tors to reach benchmark targets on state-mandated tests. She changed her methods—which featured an emphasis on varied and engaging instruc-tional activities, literacy competence, student choice, and a focus on essen-tial knowledge—to an almost exclusive focus on facts, because "facts were emphasized on [state-mandated] tests" (p. 31). The researcher who de-scribes Talbott's shift cites a principle from organizational change theory (Kanter, 1983) that is a commonplace occurrence: Employees implement practices they disagree with when faced with instability (in this case, threats or even the perception of threats such as forced transfer, loss of school ac-creditation, or just having one's name or the name of one's school listed in the newspaper).

Talbott is characterized as allowing her fear to overcome her better judg-ment, resulting in "instructional shortsightedness." Certainly, a case like Betsy Talbott's is disheartening. Her students are being shortchanged, and it is a shame. But how many Betsy Talbotts are out there? How many hun-dreds or even thousands are there? In those numbers, we have more than a disheartening situation. We have an epidemic and a catastrophe for hun-dreds of thousands of students who are made anxious and overwhelmed by too many high-stakes tests, and are made bored and disinterested by endless worksheets about trivial facts as they spend their youth learning, principally, to pass standardized tests.

Though it is not the subject of this chapter, it should still be noted that some states and accrediting agencies are taking notice and showing signs, in the form of revising teacher education program licensure standards, of supporting teachers in practicing principled instruction. In North Carolina, for example, new standards go into effect in 2009. These standards require teachers to demonstrate overt leadership in their school's governance of curriculum and the learning environment. The standards also require teachers to advocate on behalf of their students and their needs, not unlike the advocacy physicians commonly enact each day when they fight for their patients' right to have needed medical procedures paid for by their insurance companies. Actions like revising licensure standards are an encouraging sign which we hope will be supported by other efforts to minimize the undue influence—one might even call it a stranglehold—that normative grading and standardized tests currently have on educational practice. We surely cannot continue on the same path when "[I]ronically, the ineffectiveness of such practices [i.e., like those described as Betsy Talbott's 'instructional shortsightedness'] is confirmed powerfully by the very standardized test data that gave birth to them" (McTighe & Brown, 2005, p. 235).

Therefore, given the dismal scenario—so mind-numbing to students' brains, so toxic to real learning—is there an antidote? The answer, happily, is Yes. In fact, this antidote exists under many names: learning styles, cooperative learning, multiple intelligences, mind styles; in short, differentiated instruction. Tomlinson (1999, 2003), whose seminal work in this area is well known, defines differentiated instruction as "a philosophy of teaching purporting that students learn best when their teachers effectively address variance in students' readiness levels, interests, and learning profile preferences. A key goal of differentiated instruction is maximizing the learning potential of each student" (Tomlinson, 2005). Differentiated instruction is a powerful antidote to the debilitating instructional practices which have flourished under NCLB, practices which are at odds with what most educational research confirms as necessary for promoting student involvement in learning, genuine understanding of subject matter, and long-term achievement. Teaching according to differentiated instruction is supported by educational research on pedagogy (both on what works and what doesn't work) and by demographic reality. Research in the area of multicultural pedagogy is replete with information about the differences currently in play within the United States' school system as well as emerging trends:

- "Today's American society is more multilingual, multiethnic, and multicultural than any other nation in the world. For instance, it has been reported that the U.S. is comprised of at least 276 ethnic groups including 170 Native American groups" (Gollnick & Chinn, 2002, p. 15).

- "... within educational settings, by the year 2020 the majority of K–12 school children in the United States will be comprised of ethnic minority groups" (Lee, 1995, p. 6).
- "The U.S. Department of Commerce has reported that more than one-third of today's public school students are people of color. It has also been projected that, by 2025, that figure will reach 49%" (White-Clark, 2005, p. 23).

In addition to ethnic and cultural variance, students also vary in the life experience, motivation to learn, and ability level they bring to the classroom. Here are a few examples of those variances found in the literature:

- "More and more nontraditional students are being funneled into schools' most rigorous classes. Teachers are now dealing with a level of academic diversity in their classrooms which was unheard of just a decade ago" (Van Sciver, 2005, p. 37).
- Teachers with a class full of fifteen-year-olds most likely have a ten-year range of reading ability to work with (Singer & Donlan, 1989).
- "Since the 1970s the numbers of students in special education have increased by 400 percent.... In other words, for every eight children in this country in public education, one is a special education student" (Nunley, 2004, p. 9).

Research tells us that "[d]ifferentiated instruction is as important for students who find school easy as it is for those who find it difficult. All students benefit from the variety of methods... and an appropriate balance of challenge and success" (Lawrence-Brown, 2004, p. 37). Research also outlines the underpinnings of differentiated instruction, which include the following (Johnson, Johnson, Holubec, & Roy, 1984; Kolb, 1984; Krepel & Duvall, 1981; Kruse, Louis, & Bryk, 1995; Marzano, Pickering, & Pollock, 2001; Pintrich & Garcia, 1991; Reis et al., 1998; Rizzolatti, Fadiga, Fogassi, & Gallese, 1997; Sparks, 1986; Sternberg, 1997; Teaff, 1994; Tomlinson, 1999, 2003, 2005):

- Ongoing assessment, emphasizing both pre-assessment and continual formative assessment, but minimizing summative grading since too much of it is anxiety-producing
- Teaching and learning routines in various groupings (individual, small group, and whole group)
- Learning goals focused on key principles and essential knowledge of a topic or discipline, not mere facts
- Flexibility in the use of instructional strategies, time, materials, activities, and space

- Safe, supportive learning environments
- Student choice and responsibility for learning.

The foundational elements listed above work because they "emanate from the best understanding of the psychology of teaching and learning, human differences, and how the brain learns" (Tomlinson, 2005, p. 264).

Educationally focused neuroscience is a particularly exciting area of research which has developed over the last thirty years with the advent of the functional MRI. As a result of this work, numerous researchers have provided educators with neurological rationales that explain why some pedagogical strategies work best for students' brains and have also provided suggestions for practical applications in the classroom (Lakoff & Johnson, 1980; Westwater & Wolfe, 2000; Kolb & Whishaw, 1990; Markowitz & Jensen, 1999; Sylwester, 1995, 1997; Jensen, 1995, 1998, 2001; Wolfe, 2001; Levin & Levin, 1990; Sousa, 2003, 2006; Caine & Caine, 1994; Jensen & Dabney, 2000; Lozanov, 1991; Wiggins & McTighe, 1998; Sprenger, 1999; Parry & Gregory, 1998; Stein, Hardy, & Totten, 1984; Benware, 1984; Hanson, 2002; Calvin, 1996, Burgess, 2000; Brighton, 2002). In fact, "more than half of the current research in the neurosciences is about *learning* or *memory*" (King-Friedrichs, 2001, p. 78). In other words, we now have hard scientific evidence providing insights into which teaching strategies and kinds of learning activities are "brain friendly."

As it turns out, the most "brain-friendly" strategies are the same as those espoused by proponents of differentiated instruction **and** by proponents of culturally responsive instruction **and** by proponents of principled/ethical class management **and** by proponents of responsible gifted and special education **and** by proponents of authentic grading practices—those which many teachers are afraid to employ because they seem incompatible with high stakes testing. Hard science is now aligned with cognitive psychology (Bramsford, Brown, & Cocking, 2001), research findings on student achievement, and the anecdotal record of numerous teacher practitioners—a confluence of hard and soft science, of lived experience and theory. It all supports, demands, requires that teachers follow these guiding principles gleaned from the research and understand their rationales:

1. Human beings construct meaning, rather than receiving it passively.
2. Learning must be guided by generalized principles to be widely applicable and appropriate for diverse populations.
3. Experts first seek to develop an understanding of problems, and this process often involves thinking in terms of core concepts or big ideas.
4. Research on expertise suggests that superficial coverage of many topics in the domain may be a poor way to help students develop subject-matter competencies.

5. Feedback is fundamental to learning, but feedback opportunities are limited in many classrooms [because so much lower-level, close-ended questioning is practiced].
6. Many assessments measure only propositional (factual) knowledge, and never ask whether students know when, where, and why to use that knowledge.
7. Every person learns in different ways.
8. The brain is a survival organ that must be engaged by its learning environment rather than threatened or negated by it. (McTighe & Brown, 2005, p. 236)

But this is old news, some might say. Research on culturally responsive teaching is two decades old and differentiated instruction even older—three decades. If they are so great, why haven't teachers yet adopted them wholesale in classrooms across the country? Good question. First of all, let's not forget the fear factor described earlier. It is a great de-motivator, creating a hostile environment for teachers who know what principled instruction is and who want to practice it. In addition, several "practical considerations"—i.e., rationalizations—are often cited:

1. **I can't give fair grades if I allow students to express knowledge in different ways.** The response to this is that "fairness" in a diverse setting does not mean treating all students as if they were clones of each other. Instead, it means giving each student the opportunity to express learning in a preferred style or modality. To do otherwise is to construct barriers to a student's demonstration of proficiency and understanding, which is the essence of unfairness.
2. **I can't manage multilevel instruction within a standards-based environment.** The logical response here is to look to the student population. If our classrooms are full of diversity—students with disabilities, those for whom English is a second language, those with limited prerequisite skills, those with different background knowledge and experience, those with behavioral difficulties such as low motivation—perhaps we shouldn't be doubting the ability to manage multilevel, culturally responsive instruction but rather the standards-based environment so noxious to accommodating it. Please know that we are not against standards in themselves, but rather how administrators, the public, and, ultimately, teachers react to how standards are assessed by NCLB. Given their reactions (based principally on fear and the poor teaching that often results from it), we might ask ourselves if it is more sensible to manage learning up-front by providing a variety of adequate supports for learning (the kind of teaching differentiated instruction represents) than to re-teach the

same material again and again in the same way to all students with
no promise of meeting the standards anyway.

3. **I don't have time to cover all the required content *and* provide
differentiated instruction, too.** The response here is that the statement is based on a false assumption. The problem is not a lack of
time, but how the time available is used. A teacher can choose to use
classroom time to provide real-world tasks and projects that require
students to explain, compare, interpret, empathize, self-assess,
shift perspective, problem solve, experiment, investigate, decision-
make, creatively express, and evaluate through a variety of activities
matched to students' preferred learning styles. Or, a teacher can
choose to use the time in the direct instruction of innumerable
facts, test at the knowledge level, and drill endlessly on standardized
test-taking techniques. It should also be noted that the typical state
standard course of study is broad in its goals for learning, allowing
teaching professionals to determine the appropriate scope, timing,
and activities they will use to help students achieve mastery of subject
matter—far from the lock-step, surface-knowledge-intensive pacing
guides that many schools have developed and forced upon teachers
in the name of high standards and accountability. Additionally, as
Finkbeiner argues (Finkbeiner, 2002; Finkbeiner & Koplin, 2002),
since we are preparing students for 21st century living in a global
society, our curricula must be focused on creating authentic literacy
situations involving intercultural communication and which build
cooperative skills necessary to developing responsible citizens. Differentiated instruction helps teachers make this focused adjustment
from facts-centered curriculum to multicultural literacy.

Even though we've argued to dismiss some common reservations about
embracing differentiated instruction, we do want to acknowledge the reality that it is not easy work to do. It is "time-consuming, resource-intensive,
and complex" work (VanSciver, 2005, p.39) because it addresses the needs
of students inherent in culturally responsive pedagogy and in defensible
assessment and classroom management practices. At the same time, it is
a threat to the prevailing educational zeitgeist, so must work doubly hard
to demonstrate its effectiveness in an educational environment whose
standardized evaluative measures can't adequately capture differentiated
instruction's successes. It must address not only the diversity within the student population, but also the shortcomings in training, experience, and
worldview of the teacher population. By way of explanation, let us share
some statistics and observations from researchers.

While the numbers of minority students is currently over one-third of
the school population, the number of minority teachers is steadily decreas-

ing—from 12.5% Black full-time public school teachers in 1974 to 9.2% in 1990–1991, with a startling 40% of U.S. schools having no minority teachers at all (White-Clark, 2005, p.23). In addition, "pre-service experiences often do not prepare teachers for making strong connections... with people from diverse ethnic and cultural backgrounds" (Schmidt, 1999, p. 332). The result is that these "teachers have resorted to less effective measures in attempts to meet the needs of their diverse students. Often, their efforts consist of minimal, fragmented content such as discussing holidays, reading multicultural literature, or having international food fairs" (White-Clark, 2005, p. 24). Lack of experience with diverse populations has resulted in cross-cultural misunderstanding, which in turn has created emotional and behavioral problems (Salzman & D'Andrea, 2001). Like a snowball which builds from a harmless sphere to a dangerous projectile as it rolls down a hill gathering bulk and speed, lack of cultural competence on the part of teachers as they roll through the educational system's growing diversity has created, if not a dangerous, at least a disturbing tendency to create management problems when they might not otherwise exist. Overcoming the cultural divide between the teaching population and the student population may seem daunting, but it is not an impossible task. Dr. Patricia Ruggiano Schmidt (Schmidt & Salamone, 2007), a leading advocate of culturally responsible pedagogy, addresses the issue by providing guidelines for teachers in her list of best practices:

1. **High expectations**: supporting students as they develop the literacy appropriate to their ages and abilities
2. **Cultural sensitivity-reshaped curriculum:** mediated for culturally valued knowledge, connecting with the standards-based curriculum as well as individual students' cultural backgrounds
3. **Active teaching methods:** involving students in a variety of reading, writing, listening, speaking, and viewing behaviors throughout the lesson
4. **Teacher as facilitator:** presenting information, briefly giving directions, summarizing responses, and working with small groups, pairs, and individuals
5. **Student control of portions of the lesson:** the "healthy hum," talking at conversation level about the topic studied while completing assignments in small groups and pairs
6. **Instruction around groups and pairs:** low anxiety; completing assignments individually, but usually in small groups or pairs with time to share ideas and think critically about work. (p. 88)

For another population of diverse students—the gifted and talented—there are equally dismal statistics. For example, in surveys given to public school elementary teachers and private-school teachers, 61% and 54%, respectively, admitted they had no training in meeting the needs of high-achieving students (Archambault et al., 1993). Thus, these students have been systematically under-challenged.

The complexity involved in fully embracing differentiated instruction and all its related defensible practices is, as mentioned above, also complicated by systemic preferences for certain ways of expressing learning. In general, extensive use of multiple-choice and standardized testing in the U.S. favors students who prefer to be told what to do and who are successful with and enjoy memorizing facts; it also favors teachers whose pedagogy is teacher-centered (Sternberg & Zhang, 2005). This hardly seems an ideal way to educate a twenty-first century student population that will be called upon to compete in the global economy in jobs that haven't yet been invented. The principled 21st century teacher must be devoted to raising both language and cultural awareness among his/her students. It is a matter of literacy, of attaining competence, of social justice. Or, as Alfred Tatum so often invokes, "its about their lives" (2000, 2006).

Given this reality, should we embrace differentiated instruction? Of course we should—not only because what we have now isn't working, but, more importantly, because it is the principled, responsible, defensible thing to do. While teachers will have to put in some hours and effort to develop a truly functioning, student-centered learning environment based on principles of differentiated instruction, some of the heavy lifting has already been completed by educators/consultants such as Marcia Tate (2003, *Worksheets Won't Grow Dendrites: 20 Instructional Strategies That Engage the Brain: 2004, Sit & Get Won't Grow Dendrites: Professional Learning Strategies That Engage the Adult Brain*) and Kathie Nunley (2003, *A Student's Brain: The Parent/Teacher Manual* and *Layered Curriculum: The Practical Solution for Teachers with More Than One Student in Their Classroom*). Their lively workshops and how-to books are based on years of research, particularly with the educational implications of neuroscience. Their easily digestible work is full of practical ideas on how teachers can work with, not against, students' natural ways of learning. What they share about the way the brain functions correlates perfectly with the principles of differentiated instruction, culturally responsive pedagogy, authentic assessment, defensible classroom management, and adaptive strategies for a number of diverse student populations. Some of what they share seems common sense; other information they share will be surprising. Here is a sample of their neuroscience-based insights:

- Strategies such as graphic organizers, music, storytelling, metaphors are more effective than long lectures and inactivity on the part of students (Tate, 2004, pp. 24, 44, 54, 60, 80).

- The brain grows more memory cells (dendrites) from hands-on authentic experiences than from artificial learning environments. In fact, without real-world, authentic experiences, minimal learning occurs (Tate, 2004, p.98).
- "Brain-friendly" teaching strategies (Tate, 2008) match perfectly with Gardner's multiple intelligences: (a) Brainstorming and discussion (verbal/linguistic, auditory); b) drawing and artwork (spatial, kinesthetic/tactile); (c) field trips (naturalist, kinesthetic/tactile); (d) games (interpersonal, kinesthetic/tactile); (e) graphic organizers (logical-mathematical/spatial, visual/tactile); (f) humor and celebration (verbal/linguistic, auditory); (g) reciprocal teaching and cooperative learning (verbal/linguistic, auditory); (h) role plays, drama, pantomimes, and charades (bodily-kinesthetic, kinesthetic); (i) storytelling (verbal-linguistic, auditory); (j) technology (spatial, visual/tactile); (k) visualization and guided imagery (spatial, visual); (l) manipulatives, experiments, labs, and models (logical/mathematical, tactile); (m) metaphors, analogies, and similes (spatial, visual/auditory); (n) mnemonic devices (musical-rhythmic, visual/auditory); (o) movement (bodily/kinesthetic, kinesthetic); (p) music, rhythm, rhyme, and rap (musical/rhythmic, auditory); (q) project/problem-based instruction (logical/mathematical, visual/tactile); (r) visuals (spatial, visual); (s) work study and apprenticeships (interpersonal, kinesthetic); (t) writing and journals (intrapersonal, visual/tactile) (see Table 1.2, p. 18).
- Students, particularly adolescents, need 8.5 to 10 hours of sleep per night. Retaining information happens during non-REM sleep cycles that hardwire the information learned the previous day (Nunley, 2003, p. 97).
- The early start times for high schools are working in opposition to the bio-rhythms of adolescents, systematically depriving them of natural REM sleep, prompting many sleep researchers to accuse schools with early start times as guilty of child abuse (Nunley, 2003, p. 99).
- When we teach a concept in class, we should add many hooks to act as retrieval cues. For example, if we are teaching students about the explorer Cortez, we should also mention Cortez (the city in Colorado near the four corners, famous for pinto beans). This is not irrelevant or distracting, but rather a cross-reference useful for retrieval later (Nunley, 2003, p. 118).
- Moderate and severe stress harms the brain, causing neurons in the hippocampus to atrophy and die. Therefore, adding additional stress just for the sake of it in any learning situation is cruel and has no place in schools. In short, teaching against students' natural

learning styles creates unnecessary stress and should be avoided.
(Nunley, 2003, p. 122).

- Any kind of humor is a great tool to help strengthen memories be-
  cause it hooks emotion to memory. (Nunley, 2003, p. 123).
- Punishment-based management reinforces the very behaviors teachers are trying to reduce (Nunley, 2003, p. 59).
- Every time a student thinks a particular thought, it fires a specific
  neural pathway. The more the pathway is used, the easier it is to fire.
  Therefore, the more a student thinks about a particular concept
  or performs a certain skill, the easier it is to think about it or do it
  (Nunley, 2003, p. 42).
- An effective way for adults to teach young people how to appropriately respond to anger, aggression, and other hypothalamus-driven
  behavior is to model the appropriate behavior when the adult has
  his/her own hypothalamus engaged (Nunley, 2003, p. 43).
- The brain works from the bottom up (the reptilian brain) and
  schools are trying to teach at the top (the cerebral cortex). Therefore, in order to promote learning, teachers must first address the
  primitive brain—by stimulating attention and by not making it react
  defensively (Nunley, 2003, p. 75).
- Punishment is a useless and damaging technique, yet is the chief
  way we raise children, manage schools and classrooms, and run our
  society (Nunley, 2003, p. 56).
- The reason punishment persists is that it reinforces the punisher
  (Nunley, 2003, p. 58). The costs of punishment are creativity and
  higher levels of thinking (p. 61).
- Neuroscience research boils down to four principles for education:
  (a) Move students up to higher regions of the brain in day-to-day
  activities, making them accountable for what they learned, not just
  completing assignments; (b) Encourage students to engage/ pay
  attention to what they're learning by offering them choices; (c)
  Counteract the power of the reptilian brain by giving students some
  control over their learning; (d) Focus on helping students grow
  dendrites (Nunley, 2003, pp. 135–136).
- When students ask why they have to learn something, tell them that
  life is easier for the person with the most dendrites and that once
  they grow a branch, it is theirs to use for more interesting pursuits
  throughout their lives (Nunley, 2003, pp. 90–91).

Marzano, Pickering, and Pollack (2001) took a slightly different approach to identifying strategies that increase student achievement, which
can be aligned with Tate's (2003) brain-friendly strategies and Gardner's
multiple intelligences. Marzano, et al's (2001) research-based strategies for

increasing student achievement are listed below in order of average effect size (greatest to least): (a) identifying similarities and differences (Tate: metaphors, analogies, and similes; graphic organizers; Gardner: spatial, visual/auditory); (b) summarizing and note taking (Tate: brainstorming and discussing; writing and journals; Gardner: visual; tactile; verbal/linguistic; auditory); (c) reinforcing effort and providing recognition (Tate: humor and celebration; Gardner: verbal/linguistic; auditory); (d) homework and practice (All areas can be tied to *homework and practice*, since the teacher who differentiates will reinforce learning by using a variety of strategies that are brain-friendly and sensitive to multiple intelligences.); (e) nonlinguistic representations (Tate: graphic organizers; Gardner: logical-mathematical/ spatial; visual/tactile); (f) cooperative learning (Tate: reciprocal teaching and cooperative learning; Gardner: verbal/linguistic; auditory); (g) setting objectives and providing feedback (Tate: reciprocal teaching and cooperative learning; Gardner: verbal/linguistic; auditory); (h) generating and testing hypotheses (Tate: brainstorming and discussion; manipulatives, experiments, labs and models; Gardner: verbal/linguistic/auditory; logical/ mathematical; tactile);(i) cues, questions, and advance organizers (Tate: graphic organizers; storytelling; Gardner: logical-mathematical/spatial; visual/tactile).

Note: We recommend the following additional resources to teachers interested in brain-based research—Diane J. Connell (2005, *Brain-based Strategies to Reach Every Learner*); Sheryl Feinstein (2004, *Secrets of the Teenage Brain*); Michael Gurian (2005, *The Minds of Boys*); Eric Jensen (2000, *Learning with the Brain in Mind*); Mel Levine (2002, *A Mind at a Time*); John Ratey (2001, *A User's Guide to the Brain*); David Sousa (2006, *How the Brain Learns*); and Patricia Wolfe (2001, *Brain Matters, Translating research Into Classroom Practice).*

While Nunley's (2004) *Layered Curriculum* is compelling in its state-of-the-art attention to "brain-friendly" teaching strategies, hers is not the only model for differentiated instruction. Tomlinson's work is a wellspring of information and pragmatic advice for all teachers in all classrooms (Tomlinson, 1995, 1999, 2003, 2005; Tomlinson & Allan, 2000; Tomlinson & McTigue, 2000). That's the beauty of differentiation. Once a teacher understands its principles and commits to practicing them, the teacher is free to tailor his/her curriculum to the needs of his/her particular classroom of students. To help ensure success in this endeavor, some tips for managing the transition are offered by one researcher (Lawrence-Brown, 2004):

– Don't panic: Not all . . . supports will be needed for every lesson . . . .

– Don't try to do everything at once: Making changes in your classroom is something like remodeling a house. If you let yourself get overwhelmed with everything you'd like to do, you'll never get anything done.

- Gradually build a collection of materials...Potential resources include your librarian, paraprofessionals, teachers in grade levels above and below yours, special area teachers, special education teachers.

- Build upon your own strengths and talents. For example, one teacher may have a special interest in horticulture, leading him to develop projects [like] a botanical garden project...Student interests may also be reflected in such projects; ... students can be enlisted as co-developers of authentic instructional projects. (p. 58)

In the spirit of John Lennon...*All we are saying is give* [differentiated instruction] *a chance. Imagine*...a classroom rich with the sounds of music; where laughter comes easily as part of learning; where each student learns at his/her own appropriate pace, depth, and level of complexity; where authority is found in sources other than the teacher and the text; where self-selected literature or locally situated projects are used as opportunities for differentiation; where lessons and unit objectives are focused on broad, deep domain concepts; *where difference* (be it giftedness, race, learning style, or cognitive skill) *is not viewed as an exception, but instead is reconstructed as normal in the classroom community*; where teachers promote relationships that lead to mutual caring by modeling positive language and attitudes toward difference and students are affirmed in the development of their peer relationships; where teacher achievement expectations cater to the individuality of students and not to their potential to conform; where the primary goal of grading is to provide high quality feedback to parents and students to support the learning process; where the ultimate goal of classroom management is not compliance or control, but rather to provide all students with equitable opportunities to learn; where hope, and engagement, and social justice reigns, not fear. It is, in short, *the perfect norm*—what our schools and classrooms *should be*.

Accepting the challenge of effectively teaching students with many different needs is an enormous task. It seems such common sense, but if it were easy, schools would uniformly be there by now. While we can implement it initially in a reasonable period of time, it will be and must be a career-long pursuit involving adaptations in teaching practice and an evolution of classroom culture. In its real ability to leave no child behind; its liberal use of humor and camaraderie; its focus on authentic and engaging work; and its eye on social justice and freedom of choice—differentiated instruction enacts virtues which, if not uniquely American, are among our most cherished. As such, it should be as common in our children's experience as baseball and apple pie.

AUTHORS' NOTES

Adopting differentiated instruction may seem, at first, to be an impossible task. Some teachers, particularly those new to the profession and pre-service candidates, may feel overwhelmed by what appear to be a dizzying array of pedagogical choices, theories, and focuses of instruction. Yet, if we step back and look at the foundational principles involved—the core principles and essential knowledge of differentiated instruction—we quickly see that differentiated instruction fits like hand in glove with Gardner's multiple intelligences, "brain-friendly" teaching strategies, educational implications of research in cognitive psychology and neuroscience, and culturally responsive pedagogy. In addition, differentiated instruction is aligned with practices of defensible assessment and ethical classroom management. Tables 1.1 and 1.2 (which reiterate information presented earlier in this chapter) illustrate the confluence of all this research and theory.

TABLE 1.1

	Principles of differentiated instruction	Principles of cognitive psychology and neuroscience research	Principles of culturally responsive pedagogy	Principles of defensible assessment and ethical management
Goals	Learning goals focused on key principles and essential knowledge, not mere facts	Learning must be guided by general principles to be widely applicable for a diverse population; experts think in terms of core principles	High expectations, supporting students as they develop the literacy appropriate to their ages and abilities	Assessment should be criterion-based and developed with student learning outcomes in mind
Engagement in learning	Student choice and responsibility for learning	Human beings construct meaning rather than receive it passively	Student control of portions of lessons	When students are engaged in learning, they do not create management problems
Teaching and learning	Teaching and learning routines in various groupings	Every person learns in different ways	Instruction around groups and pairs (low anxiety)	Students differ in how they best demonstrate learning (e.g., some perform

	Principles of differentiated instruction	Principles of cognitive psychology and neuroscience research	Principles of culturally responsive pedagogy	Principles of defensible assessment and ethical management
				better on multiple choice tests, while some perform better on projects).
Instructional strategies	Flexibility in instructional strategies, time, materials, and activities	Every person learns in different ways; hence, offer variety	Active teaching methods; teacher is facilitator	Like instructional strategies, diverse approaches to assessment are necessary for students to show what they know and can do. Assessment should reflect the intended student learning outcome.
Environment	Safe, supportive learning environment	The brain is a survival organ that must be engaged by the learning environment rather than threatened or negated by it	Active teaching methods, during which teacher is a facilitator	When students are learning in ways that are positive and comfortable for them, they will succeed and will cause fewer problems in the classroom.
Assessment	Ongoing assessment, minimizing summative assessment and focusing on pre-assessment and continuing formative assessment	Feedback is fundamental to learning; need to measure more than factual learning	Assessment must reflect sensitivity to learning differences. The teacher must be cognizant of cultural bias in testing.	Teachers should not focus on teaching to the test

Table 1.2 shows the correlation between research-based, "brain-friendly" teaching strategies and Gardner's multiple intelligences (Tate, 2003). We have put these in a table with Marzano's (see Marzano, Pickering, & Pollack, 2001) research-based strategies for increasing student achievement. Marzano's strategies are different from the other two in that many of Marzano's can be aligned with Tate's and Gardner's, depending on how you implement, for example, *homework and practice,* or if a game has students *identifying similarities and differences.* In other words, you may see other ways Marzano's strategies can be aligned, but not agree with the way we have done so.

It is also easy to see how using a variety of "brain-friendly" teaching strategies in your classroom follow the principles of differentiated instruction and culturally responsive teaching—with their focus on student-centeredness, engagement, and flexibility in instructional strategies—which are listed in Table 1.1.

TABLE 1.2

Brain-friendly teaching strategy	Gardner's multiple intelligences	Marzano's strategies for increasing student achievement
Brainstorming and discussion	Verbal-linguistic; auditory	Generating and testing hypotheses
Drawing and artwork	Spatial; kinesthetic/tactile	Nonlinguistic
Field trips	Naturalist; kinesthetic/tactile	Nonlinguistic
Games	Interpersonal; kinesthetic/tactile	Setting objectives and providing feedback; cooperative learning; homework and practice; reinforcing effort and providing recognition; identifying similarities and differences
Graphic organizers	Logical-mathematical/spatial; visual/tactile	Nonlinguistic; questions, cues, and advance organizers; identifying similarities and differences
Humor and celebration	Verbal-linguistic; auditory	Reinforcing effort and providing recognition
Reciprocal teaching and cooperative learning	Verbal-linguistic; auditory	Cooperative learning
Role plays, drama, pantomimes, and charades	Bodily-kinesthetic; kinesthetic	Nonlinguistic
Storytelling	Verbal-linguistic; auditory	Generating and testing hypotheses; homework and practice; cooperative learning; identifying similarities and differences; summarizing and note taking; questions, cues and advance organizers

Brain-friendly teaching strategy	Gardner's multiple intelligences	Marzano's strategies for increasing student achievement
Technology	Spatial; visual/tactile	Generating and testing hypotheses; homework and practice; cooperative learning; identifying similarities and differences; summarizing and note taking; questions, cues and advance organizers; nonlinguistic
Visualization and guided imagery	Spatial; visual	Nonlinguistic
Manipulatives, experiments, labs, and models	Logical-mathematical; tactile	Nonlinguistic
Metaphors, analogies, and similes	Spatial; visual/auditory	Identifying similarities and differences
Mnemonic devices	Musical-rhythmic; visual/auditory	Questions, cues and advance organizers
Movement	Bodily-kinesthetic; kinesthetic	Nonlinguistic; cooperative learning; homework and practice; questions, cues and advance organizers
Music, rhythm, rhyme, and rap	Musical-rhythmic; auditory	Identifying similarities and differences; questions, cues and advance organizers; reinforcing effort and providing recognition
Project/problem-based instruction	Logical-mathematical; visual/tactile	Generating and testing hypotheses
Visuals	Spatial; visual	Identifying similarities and differences; nonlinguistic
Work study, action research, and apprenticeships	Interpersonal; kinesthetic	Generating and testing hypotheses; homework and practice
Writing and reflecting	Intrapersonal; visual/tactile	Summarizing and note taking

WORKS CITED

Archambault, F. X., Jr., Westberg, K. L., Brown, S., Hallmark, B. W., Zhang, W., & Emmons, C. (1993). Classroom practices used with gifted third and fourth grade students. *Journal of the Education of the Gifted, 16*(2), 103–119.

Baglieri, S., & Knopf, J. H. (2004, November/December). Normalizing difference in inclusive teaching. *Journal of Learning Disabilities, 37*(6), 525–529.

Bejoian, L. M., & Reid, D. K. (2005) A disability studies perspective on the Bush education agenda: The No Child Left Behind Act of 2001. *Equity and Excellence in Education, 4*(3), 512–532.

Benware, D. (1984). The quality of learning with an active versus passive motivational set. *American Educational Research Journal, 21,* 755–765.

Bramsford, J., Brown, I., & Cocking, R. (2001). *How people learn: Brain, mind experience and school.* Washington, DC: National Research Council.

Brighton, C. M. (2002, Summer). Straddling the fence: Implementing best practices in an age of accountability. *Gifted Child Today Magazine, 25*(3), 30–33.

Burgess, R. (2000). *Laughing lessons: 149 2/3 ways to make teaching and learning fun.* Minneapolis, MN: Free Spirit.

Caine, R. N., & Caine, G. (1994). *Making connections: Teaching and the human brain.* Menlo Park, CA: Addison-Wesley.

Calvin, W. (1996). *How brains think.* New York: Basic Books.

Cartledge, G., & Milburn, J. F. (1996). *Cultural diversity and social skills instruction: Understanding ethnic and gender differences.* Champaign, IL: Research Press.

Connell, D.J. (2005). *Brain-based strategies to reach every learner.* New York: Scholastic Books.

Dobbs, M. (2004, December 7). In a global test of math skills, U.S. students behind the curve. *The Washington Post,* A1, A8.

Feinstein, S. (2004). *Secrets of the teenage brain.* Thousand Oaks, CA: Corwin Press.

Finkbeiner, C. (2002). Foreign language practice and cooperative learning. In C. Finkbeiner (Ed.) *Wholeheartedly English: A life of learning.* Berlin: Cornelson, 109–122.

Finkbeiner, C., & Koplin, C. (2002). A cooperative approach for facilitating intercultural education. *Reading Online,* 6(3). Newark, DE: International Reading Association.

Gollnick, D. M., & Chinn, P. C. (2002). *Multicultural education in a pluralistic society* (6th ed.). Upper Saddle River, NJ: Merrill Prentice Hall.

Gurian, M. (2005). *The minds of boys.* San Francisco, CA: Jossey-Bass.

Guskey, T., & Bailey, J. (2001). *Developing grading and reporting systems for student learning.* Thousand Oaks, CA: Corwin.

Hanson, A. (2002). *Write brain write.* San Diego, CA: The Brain Store.

Irvine, J. J. (1990). *Black students and school failure: Policies, practices, and prescriptions.* New York: Greenwood.

Jensen, E. (1995). *The learning brain.* Del Mar, CA: The Brain Store.

Jensen, E. (1998). *Sizzle and substance: Presenting with the brain in mind.* San Diego, CA: The Brain Store.

Jensen, E. (2000). *Learning with the brain in mind.* San Diego, CA: The Brain Store.

Jensen, E. (2001). *Arts with the brain in mind.* Alexandria, VA: Association for Supervision and Curriculum Development.

Jensen, E., & Dabney, M. (2000). *Learning smarter: The new science of teaching.* San Diego, CA: The Brain Store.

Johnson, D., Johnson, R. T., Holubec, E. J., & Roy, P. (1984). *Circles of learning: Cooperation in the classroom.* Alexandria, VA: Association for Supervision and Curriculum Development.

Kanter, R. M. (1983). *The change masters: Innovations for productivity in the American corporation.* New York: Simon & Shuster.

King-Friedrichs, J. (2001, November). Brain-friendly techniques for improving memory. *Educational Leadership, 59* (3), 76–79.

Kolb, D. (1984). *Experiential learning: Experience as the source of learning and Development.* Englewood Cliffs, NJ: Prentice Hall.

Kolb, B., & Whishaw, I. Q. (1990). *Fundamentals of human neuropsychology.* New York: W.H. Freeman.

Krepel, W. J., & Duvall, C. R. (1981). *Field trips: A guide for planning and conducting educational experiences.* Washington, DC: National Education Association.

Kruse, S. D., Louis, K. S., & Bryk, A. (1995). An emerging framework for analyzing school-based professional community. In K. S. Lewis & S. D. Kruse (Eds.), *Professionalism and community: Perspectives on reforming urban schools.* (pp. 23–42). Thousand Oaks, CA: Corwin Press

Lakoff, G., & Johnson, M. (1980). *Metaphors we live by.* University of Chicago Press.

Lawrence-Brown, D. (2004, Summer). Differentiated instruction: Inclusive strategies for standards-based learning that benefit the whole class. *American Secondary Education, 32*(3), 34–63.

Lee, C. C. (1995). *Counseling for diversity: A guide for school counselors and related Professionals.* Boston, MA: Allyn & Bacon.

Levin, M. E., & Levin, J. R. (1990). Scientific mnemonomies: Methods for maximizing more than memory. *American Educational Research Journal, 27,* 301–321.

Levine, M. (2002). *A mind at a time.* New York: Simon & Schuster.

Lozanov, G. (1991). On some problems of the anatomy, physiology, and biochemistry of cerebral activities in the global-artistic approach in modern pedagogic training. *Journal of the Society for Accelerative Learning and Teaching, 16,* 101–116.

Markowitz, K., & Jensen, E. (1999). *The great memory book.* San Diego, CA: The Brain Store.

Marzano, R. J., Pickering, D. J., & Pollack, J. E. (2001). *Classroom instruction that works.* Alexandria, VA: Association for Supervision and Curriculum Development.

McTighe, J., & Brown, J. L. (2005). Differentiated instruction and educational standards: Is détente possible? *Theory into Practice, 44*(3), 234–244.

National Center for Educational Statistics (2002). *NAEP writing results.* Retrieved Nov. 20, 2007, from http://www.nces.ed.gov/reportcard/writing/results2002.

No Child Left Behind Act of 2001, Pub. L. No. 107-110. (2002).

Nunley, K. F. (2003). *A student's brain: The parent/ teacher manual.* Kearney, NE: Morris.

Nunley, K. F. (2004). *Layered curriculum: The practical solution for teachers with more than one student in their classroom* (2e). Kearney, NE: Morris.

O'Connor, K. (2002). *How to grade for learning: Linking grades to standards* (2e). Arlington Heights, IL: Skylight.

Parry, T., & Gregory, G. (1998). *Designing brain-compatible learning.* Arlington Heights, IL: Skylight.

Pintrich, J., & Garcia, T. (1991). Student goal orientation and self-regulation in the college classroom. In M. Maher & J. Pint rich (Eds.), *Advances in motivation and achievement 7* (pp. 371–402). Greenwich, CT: JAI,.

Ratey, J. J. (2001). *A user's guide to the brain.* New York: Vintage Books.

Reis, S.M., Kaplan, S. N., Tomlinson, C. A., Westberg, K. L., Callahan, C. M., & Cooper, C. R. (1998, November). Equal does not mean identical. *Educational Leadership,* 74–77.

Rizzolatti, G., Fadiga, L., Fogassi, L., & Gallese, V. (1997). Enhance: The space around us. *Science, 277,* 190–191.

Salzman, M., & D'Andrea, M. (2001). Assessing the impact of a prejudice prevention project. *Journal of Counseling and Development, 79,* 341–346.

Schmidt, P. R. (1999, March). Focus on research: Know thyself and understand others. *Language Arts, 76* (4), 332–339.

Schmidt, P. R. (2003). *Culturally relevant pedagogy: A study of successful in-service.*

Schmidt, P. R., & Salamone, K. (2007). Closing the gap with culturally relevant pedagogy in the urban English classroom. In K.K. Jackson & S. Vavra (Eds.), *Closing the gap: English educators address the tensions between teacher preparation and teaching in secondary schools,* (87–112). Charlotte, NC: Information Age.

Singer, H., & Donlan, D. (1989). *Reading and learning from text.* Hillsdale, NJ: Erlbaum.

Sousa, D. (2006). *How the brain learns.* Thousand Oaks, CA: Corwin Press.

Sousa, D. (2003). *How the gifted brain learns.* Thousand Oaks, CA: Corwin Press.

Sparks, G. (1986). The effectiveness of alternative training activities in changing school practices. *American Educational Journal, 23*(2), 217–225.

Sprenger, M. (1999). *Learning and memory: The brain in action.* Alexandria, VA: Association for Supervision and Curriculum Development.

Stein, B., Hardy, C. A., & Totten, H. (1984). The use of music and imagery to enhance and accelerate information retention. *Journal of the Society for Accelerative Learning and Teaching, 7*(4).

Sternberg, J. (1997). *Successful intelligence: How practical and creative intelligence determine success in life.* New York: First Plume.

Sternberg R. J., & Zhang, L. (2005). Styles of thinking as a basis of differentiated instruction. *Theory into Practice, 44*(3), 245–253.

Sylwester, R. (1995). *A celebration of neurons: An educator's guide to the brain.* Alexandria, VA: Association for Supervision and Curriculum Development.

Sylwester, R. (1997). The neurobiology of self-esteem and aggression. *Educational Leadership, 54,* 75–79.

Tate, M. (2003). *Worksheets don't grow dendrites: 20 instructional strategies that engage the brain.* Thousand Oaks, CA: Corwin Press.

Tate, M. (2004). *"Sit and get" won't grow dendrites: Professional learning strategies that engage the adult brain.* Thousand Oaks, CA: Corwin Press.

Tatum, A.W. (2000). Breaking down barriers that disenfranchise African-American adolescent readers in low-level tracks. *Journal of Adolescent and Adult Literacy, 44*(1), 52–64.

Tatum, A.W. (2006). Engaging African-American males in reading. *Educational Leadership, 63*(5), 44–49.

Teaff, G. (1994). *Coaching in the classroom: Teaching self-motivation.* Waco, TX: Cord Communications.

Tomlinson, C. A. (1995). *How to differentiate instruction in mixed-ability classrooms.* Alexandria, VA: Association for Supervision and Curriculum Development.

Tomlinson, C. A. (1999). *The differentiated classroom: Responding to the needs of all learners.* Alexandria, VA: Association for Supervision and Curriculum Development.

Tomlinson, C. A. (2003). *Fulfilling the promise of the differentiated classroom: Tools and strategies for responsive teaching.* Alexandria, VA: Association for Supervision and Curriculum Development.

Tomlinson, C. A. (2005). Grading and differentiation: Paradox or good practice? *Theory into Practice, 44*(3), 262–269.

Tomlinson, C., & Allan, S. (2000). Leadership for differentiation schools and classrooms. Alexandria, VA: Association for Supervision and Curriculum Development.

Tomlinson, C., & McTighe, J. (2000). *Understanding by design and differentiated instruction: Two models for student success.* Alexandria, VA: Association for Supervision and Curriculum Development.

VanSciver, J. H. (2005, May). NCLB fitfully fits differentiated instruction. *Education Digest: Essential Readings Condensed for Quick Review, 70*(9), 37–39.

Weinstein, C., Curran, M., & Tomlinson-Clarke, S. (2003, Autumn). Culturally responsive classroom management: Awareness into action. *Theory into Practice, 42*(4), 269–276.

Westwater, A., & Wolfe, P. (2000). The brain-compatible curriculum. *Educational Leadership, 58*(3), 49–52.

White-Clark, R. (2005, April). Training teachers to succeed in a multicultural classroom. *The Education Digest: Essential Readings Condensed for Quick Review, 70*(8), 23–26.

Wiggins, G. (1993). *Assessing student performances.* San Francisco: Jossey-Bass.

Wiggins, G., & McTighe, J. (1998). *Understanding by design.* Alexandria, VA: Association for Supervision and Curriculum Development.

Wink, J. (2000). *Critical pedagogy: Notes from the real world* (2e). New York: Addison Wesley Longman.

Wolfe, P. (2001). *Brain matters: Translating research into classroom practice.* Alexandria, VA: Association for Supervision and Curriculum Development.

CHAPTER 2

THE FABRIC OF MY LIFE

Using Poetry, Prose, and Graphic Novels to Help Students Reflect Upon Their Identities

INTRODUCTION

There is no other time in our lives when exploring who we are, who we are in our family and world, and who we will be is stronger than during adolescence and young adulthood. Teachers can use the intense focus on self with middle and high school age students because they are a rich spring from which to draw deep emotions and sharp insights.

Knowledge of self is a creative force just like a river is in nature. Rivers wind their way through mountains and valleys, carving away at the rocks and earth that surround them—both impacting and impacted by those elements. It is the individual river flowing from each student that teachers seek to understand and then help find its path. Just like natural elements channel a river's course, this unit uses four essential questions to channel students' reflections on identity:

- Who am I?: The voice within
- Where do I come from?: The voice of the past
- How do I fit within the world?: The voice of the present
- What are my hopes and aspirations?: The voice of the future

In this unit, *voice* means three things. The first is what each student must find within him/herself—the words, the thoughts, the pieces students put together to find their identity. Second, *voice* means that each student has a "say" in how he/she chooses to represent the *voice* within. Therefore, while some assignments are required, each student has some choice about how to meet particular objectives. Thus, students may write a poem or song, create a photo story, or sew a quilt to represent different aspects of self. Finally, the activities in this unit are designed to encourage the development of a strong writing *voice*, one that conveys the person behind the writing as authentic and competent. While developing a writing voice is important to this unit, it should be emphasized that all the language arts (literacy skills) have been incorporated, not just reading and writing.

About the time that I was working on this unit, I was reading the graphic novel *Maus*, and its sequel, *Maus II,* by Art Spiegelman. Graphic novels are so popular today, as is comic drawing. My daughter has read numerous graphic novels, although few are the quality of *Maus*, and both of my children have taken comic design workshops as middle school electives and in summer camp settings. In fact, comic design was so popular among middle school students that at least one week-long section, if not two, was offered for each of the eight weeks of summer camp. *Maus* was selected as the seminal work from which to develop their unique stories in this unit.

It was in reading the *Maus* books that I knew I wanted students to have an opportunity to experience one man's story (or maybe two men's stories—Artie's and his dad's) as a way of seeing relationships, imagery, and dialogue as the primary means of conveying the story. And because *The Fabric of My Life* is about students' own stories and relationships—whether written as poetry, prose, or in a graphic novel format—these graphic novels fit the unit perfectly.

Of course, "brain-friendly" strategies are always on my mind in planning. So, naturally, there are lots of art and music opportunities, cooperative learning/peer teaching (lyric circles and editing teams), brainstorming and discussion, journaling and reflecting, and, if you think flexibly, you can count the focused trip home as a "fieldtrip" in which students record sounds, images, and ideas. Of course, technology comes into play with "publishing" their work, as well as in representations and presentations (photo stories; PowerPoint; researching lyrics and songs; bringing in their iPods, MP3 players, or CDs). Finally, storytelling is an obvious "brain-friendly" technique in this unit. Students will be given opportunities to visualize what they are hearing and what it means to them.

Although the relationship of theories and research has already been discussed in the first chapter, it is important to note that this unit reflects culturally responsive pedagogy. First, the teacher is a facilitator with high expectations, helping each student as he/she develops the literacy appropriate to his/her age and ability. The methods employed are active; students often work in groups and pairs, reducing anxiety. Students have control over certain portions of the lesson, in how they choose to demonstrate their learning. Finally, and most significantly, this unit values each student's cultural background and allows each student to share a part of him- or herself in each activity.

Always in the back of my mind are the standards and objectives expected at each grade level. State curriculum standards closely align with national/international standards—in this case, the North Carolina Standard Course of Study (NCSCOS) for English/Language Arts with those set forth by the National Council for Teachers of English/International Reading Association (NCTE-IRA). Ninth grade was selected as the target audience for this unit for two main reasons. First, the ninth grade curriculum typically focuses on genre study, while continuing to develop in the communication skills of speaking, listening, reading, writing, and use of media and technology (visual literacy). In this process, ninth grade students become more proficient in grammar and language usage and knowing when to use formal versus informal language, depending on the purpose and audience. Second, exploring themselves and others through a variety of genre and media seemed like a wonderful transition into high school. In the national/international standards (NCTE-IRA), it is a time for gaining deep understandings of self and others along cultural, ethical, philosophical, social, and aesthetic dimensions.

STUDENT LEARNING OUTCOMES

1. Given a format and an example, students will write and share poems about self. (Bio-poem, Who Am I?)
2. After listening to poems used as examples or written by others in the class, students will identify personally memorable images which helped them learn something new about the author of the poem.
3. After listening to lyrics (e.g., *Tapestry* by Carole King; *Small Town* by John Mellencamp), students will discuss the meaning conveyed in the lyrics and how the music influences the meaning.
4. Given examples of lyrics, students will research and share published lyrics that represent them in "lyric circles."
5. Using sample and original poems and lyrics, students will identify colorful language, vivid images, and metaphors, similes, analogies used to create the tone and meaning of the writing.
6. By keeping a journal, students will record images: sounds, smells, sight, touch, taste.
7. After reading sample "This I Believe" essays, students will write one and, once edited, submit it to a particular website.
8. After writing a first draft (of each type of writing in the unit), students will work with partners to edit each piece using a guided editing tool.
9. Given models, students will identify examples in their work of when formal grammar and language usage (vs. informal usage) can/cannot be used to convey the message/create the desired effect.
10. After reading and discussing *Maus* and *Maus II* by Art Spiegelman, students will draw at least four pictures in a sequence and write conversation and captions to carry the story.
11. Provided with options, students will visually or musically represent (e.g., make a quilt, paint a mural, write/perform a song, create a media presentation/photo story with music) each of the four essential questions for the unit.

OVERVIEW OF THE UNIT

This unit uses a layered curriculum approach (Nunley, 2004). Here is a quick review of layered curriculum: The "C" layer builds upon students' existing knowledge, laying a common foundation for understanding. In this unit, students write poems using models and comprehend lyrics, essays, and stories. In the "B" layer, students analyze and apply their knowledge and understanding by selecting and writing poems, lyrics, and essays that represent them. In layer "A," students evaluate and create; in this unit, they write poems about themselves, evaluate similarities and differences in essays, craft their own stories as graphic novelettes, and choose visual, oral, and written ways to demonstrate who they are in a final project. The table below provides a visual map of the unit, identifying the sub-units and the activities in each sub-unit at each layer. The numbers in parentheses indicate the days on which a particular activity occurs (e.g., writing the Who am I? poem occurs on day 3).

Four essential questions (sub-units)	Layer C Know and comprehend	Layer B Apply and analyze	Layer A Evaluate and create
Who am I?: The voice within	Biopoem (1) Images journal (2–3) *Tapestry* (2)	*Who Am I?* poem (3)	Poetry collection *(assigned day 3)*
Where do I come from?: The voice of the past	*Small town* (4) *Maus* and *Maus II* (5–10)	Choice writing and visual representation (4)	Personal mini graphic novel (11–13)
How do I fit within the world?: The voice of the present	Read/discuss sample *This I Believe* essays (14–15)	*This I Believe* essay (16–17) Lyrics project (3, 18–19)	*This I Believe* collections (20)
What are my hopes and aspirations?: The voice of the future			Final project–written and creative choices (20)

What follows are the prompts and rubrics as indicated for each activity on the graphic organizer above, by day. As you will note, some activities take more than one day.

WHO AM I?: THE VOICE WITHIN

Day 1: Biopoems

Student Learning Outcomes for this Activity

- Given a bio-poem format and an example, students will write and share bio-poems about self.
- After listening to poems used as examples or written by others in the class, students will identify personally memorable images which helped them learn something new about the author of the poem.

Note: Give students a handout for each activity which includes the prompt, a model/sample (where appropriate), and the rubric that will be used to assess their work. A list of websites for graphic organizers is provided at the end of the unit.

Prompt: Introduce yourself through a Bio-poem. Follow the form of the sample Bio-poem below. Remember: your Bio-poem can be whatever length you want it to be. It doesn't have to be thirteen lines long, and you don't have to include exactly three ideas in any of the lines. The form is a simple guideline. Make sure that you do use words that are descriptive, colorful and lively. It should be YOUR creative expression about YOU.

Suggested Bio-Poem Form

Line 1: Your first name
Line 2: Who is . . . (Descriptive words that describe you)
Line 3: Who is brother or sister of . . .
Line 4: Who loves . . . (three ideas or people)
Line 5: Who feels . . . (three ideas)
Line 6: Who needs . . . (three ideas)
Line 7: Who gives . . . (three ideas)
Line 8: Who fears . . . (three ideas)
Line 9: Who would like to see . . .
Line 10: Who shares . . .
Line 11: Who is . . .
Line 12: Who is a resident of . . .
Line 13: Your last name

For more information on Bio-poems see http://www.seedsofknowledge.com/biopoems.html.

Prompt:

- Write bio-poems individually.
- Share poems in teams of 4 or 5. Discuss what you learned about each other after each reads his/her poem.
- Display the written poems in the classroom.

Rubric: Poetry and Lyrics

	Exemplary	Effective	Acceptable	Unacceptable
Format	Used suggested format effectively to communicate ideas creatively	Used format as a vehicle for communicating ideas	Used format rigidly, sometimes awkwardly	Did not use format, but had some ideas written
Flow	Writing flowed smoothly and rhythmically throughout	Writing flowed smoothly, or rhythmically	Writing flowed fairly smoothly, although some lines may have seemed awkward	Writing was choppy and awkward — did not flow smoothly
Word choice	Words are carefully selected, creating vivid images and insights about the student	Words are carefully selected and clearly provides insights about the student	Words selected often, but not always, provide insights about the student	Words do not appear to be carefully selected; rather, they appear merely to complete the assignment

Day 2: Tapestry

Student Learning Outcomes:
- After listening to lyrics (*Tapestry* by Carole King), students will discuss the meaning conveyed in the lyrics and how the music influences the meaning of each.
- Using sample and original poems and lyrics, students will identify colorful language, vivid images, metaphors, similes, analogies used to create the tone and meaning of the writing.
- By keeping a journal, students will record images: sounds, smells, sight, touch, taste.

Prompt:
- Lyrics are poetry and expressions of feelings and images.
- Listen to *Tapestry* by Carol King on audiotape, iPod, or CD; read the lyrics, which the instructor will distribute. The lyrics are available at www.caroleking.com.
- Individually, write your general impressions of *Tapestry*. What does it say to you? How does it make you feel? What does it make you think of?
- In teams, share what you wrote and discuss general impressions.
- In teams, draw and discuss an assigned stanza.
- Be prepared to share drawing(s) and discussion points with class.

Rubric: Draw and Discuss an Assigned Stanza

	Exemplary	Effective	Acceptable	Unacceptable
Drawing	Significant images represent the song's words fully and are integrated as a conceptual whole, in a highly creative manner	Significant images represent the song's words fully and are integrated as a conceptual whole	Many significant images represent the song's words and are somewhat integrated as a conceptual whole	Some images represent the song's words, but are not presented as a connected or integrated whole
Discussion points	Demonstrates clear, consistent, reflective thinking and understanding	Demonstrates clear, consistent thinking and understanding	Demonstrates clear understanding	Demonstrates limited understanding

Mini-Lesson on Metaphors, Similes and Analogies

Prompt:
- Create a Foldable® with 3 pockets, labeling each pocket as shown below. After looking up the definitions, write the definition for each in your own words on a card to slip in the appropriate pocket for reference.

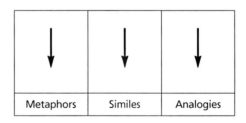

The following website defines these three terms and provides some examples. http://ask.yahoo.com/20030623.html

- Individually, sort the strips with examples of metaphors, similes, and analogies into the pockets.
- In teams, discuss categories, definitions, and examples of each and re-sort as needed.
- Add metaphors, analogies, similes from *Tapestry*.
- Write original metaphors, analogies, similes.

Rubric: Metaphors, Similes, and Analogies

	Exemplary	Effective	Acceptable	Minimal
Identifying and writing metaphors, similes, and analogies	Can sort independently and write several examples of each . . . some of which are clearly creative	Can sort independently and write good examples of each	Can sort with minimal assistance and write a basic example of each	Can sort with assistance, but has difficulty writing examples

Images Journal

Student Learning Outcome:
- By keeping a journal, students will record images: sounds, smells, sight, touch, taste.

Prompt:

What are the tastes, textures, and aromas of your life? On the way home from school and at home, notice the smells, sounds, sights, tastes and feel of the things around you. How do you perceive your world? What makes you "you?" Write these things down as words or phrases that capture the images, smells, sounds. Use descriptive words to communicate the essence of your world. Use *metaphors, analogies, and similes*, as they come to you in writing these phrases or by connecting two phrases. Draw sketches that capture significant images, whether actual or those created in your mind.

Examples:

trees—like tall men, both thick and thin, waving their arms in the wind; like soldiers at attention, the lights on the poles stood over the city; the bright purple blossoms of the redbud; chirping of birds; new bright green leaves on trees; sun, like a warm blanket embracing you; the lavender wisteria drapes over the trees.

Day 3: Writing *"Who Am I?"* Poems

Student Learning Outcomes

- From their individual journals, students will share and chart images: sounds, smells, sight, touch, taste.
- Given a format and an example, students will write and share poems about self. (Bio-poem, Who Am I?)
- After listening to poems used as examples or written by others in the class, students will identify personally memorable images that helped them learn something new about the author of the poem.

Prompt:

In teams, share tastes, textures, and aromas of your lives from the homework assignment. Record journal entries on the chart below that are common to three or more team members' journals and those entries that are unique to only one. Report out to class.

	Common to 3 or more	Unique to 1
Smells		
Sounds		
Sights		
Tastes		
Textures		
Other		

Prompt:

Introduce *How to Write an I Am Poem* (from www.CanTeach.ca).

Like bio-poems, *I Am* and *Who Am I?* poems allow students to focus on themselves and what makes them unique. These types of poems are great as beginning-of-the-year icebreakers. They also provide formulaic writing opportunities to "warm up" to poetry writing. The form and examples are provided below:

I Am

I am (two special characteristics)
I wonder (something you are actually curious about)
I hear (an imaginary sound)
I see (an imaginary sight)
I want (an actual desire)
I am (the first line of the poem restated)

I pretend (something you actually pretend to do)
I feel (a feeling about something imaginary)
I touch (an imaginary touch)
I worry (something that really bothers you)
I cry (something that makes you very sad)
I am (the first line of the poem repeated)

I understand (something you know is true)
I say (something you believe in)
I dream (something you actually dream about)
I try (something you really make an effort about)
I hope (something you actually hope for)
I am (the first line of the poem repeated)

http://www.bbc.co.uk/wales/southwest/sites/poetry/pages/anita_wakeham
.shtml (This site also has a sample poem.)

Who Am I? poems
(Written by Sharon L. Spencer, following the models provided above.)

Who Am I?

I am sensitive, yet strong
I wonder how this came to be
I hear subtle emotions in others' words
I see falsehoods
I want honesty from others
I am sensitive, yet strong

I pretend I do not hear these things
I feel a sense of sadness
I touch a deep knowledge that has no words
I worry about my perceptions
I cry with the heaviness of this understanding
I am sensitive, yet strong

I understand that we must have faith
I say there is hope
I dream that we can show mutual respect for others
I try to instill a sense of trust
I hope for peace, honesty, and understanding
I am sensitive, yet strong.

Who Am I?

Who Am I? I am Cancer,
not the disease, but the crab.
But sometimes it feels like the disease. . .
With its dark and gloomy mood
that makes me retreat into my shell.

Other times, I scurry sideways
Avoiding direct conflict,
But that does not really preserve me.
It makes me feel dark and gloomy
wanting, again, to hide in my shell.

Yet, sometimes, the world is bright
and it is quite beautiful.
The sun flickers between the leaves on the trees
And the world seems peaceful and warm.
I want to bask in it for a long time.

With Scorpio rising, I am all water
And, sometimes, more often than I wish,
The dam lets loose, and the water
gushes out fast and furious, expressing emotions,
whether happy or sad, in a sea of tears.

I Am

I am like the weather
Sometimes I am dark and stormy
And the skies are gloomy and gray
Sometimes I see the glorious sunlight
flickering through the trees
as I drive down a country road
The town, in the distance,
stands tall against clear blue skies.

Prompt:
- Identify metaphors, similes, and analogies in *Who Am I?* poem examples above and in own original poems.

Rubrics:
- Use poetry rubric (from Day 1) for poems written.
- Use metaphors, similes and analogies rubric (from Day 2).

Lyric Circles

Student Learning Outcomes
- Given examples of lyrics, students will research and share published lyrics that represent them in "lyric circles."
- Using poems and lyrics, students will identify colorful language, vivid images, metaphors, similes, analogies used to create the tone and meaning of the writing.

Prompt:
- Bring in lyrics that evoke a strong feeling or sense of identity – lyrics that speak to you personally.
- In teams, share lyrics (and music, if available).
- Discuss what words or phrases really "grab" you. For each team member in your lyric circle, record ideas on the chart below. This will provide a growing list of words, thoughts, ideas that evoke images, along with students' journal entries and images gleaned from poems. Team charts will be shared with the class.

Team Member	Song Titles	How/why it speaks to you	Images, words, phrases, etc.

Optional/ Challenge Assignment:

Research different poetry types (e.g., ballad, lyric, sonnet, epic, narrative). Choose at least two different types, and write at least five additional poems that are about you. Put these in a booklet or catalog for sharing and display; include pictures or designs to enhance the visual presentation.

"WHO AM I IN MY FAMILY?" OR, "WHERE DID I COME FROM?"

Day 4: Small Town

Student Learning Outcomes:
- After listening to lyrics (*Small Town* by John Mellencamp), students will discuss the meaning conveyed in the lyrics and how the music influences the meaning of each.
- Using sample and original poems and lyrics, students will identify colorful language, vivid images, metaphors, similes, analogies used to create the tone and meaning of the writing.

Prompt:
1. Discuss lyrics in teams. (Develop questions.) Lyric available on the website (http://www.songfacts.com/detail.php?id=669). The song

can be heard on the web as well (http//:www.vh1classic.com/view/ artist/ 12334/172032/John_Mellencamp/Small_Town/index.jhtml)
2. In teams, identify metaphors, similes, analogies, or images in the song and record in individual student journals.
3. Write a poem, lyrics, or narrative about where you came from, about your family and about your place within the family.
4. Represent these things by putting together images (e.g., a collage, a photo album, a photo story on the computer).

Rubric:
   Use poetry/lyrics rubric (from Day 1).

Day 5–10: Maus

Student Learning Outcomes
- After reading *Maus* and *Maus II,* graphic novels by Art Spiegelman, students will draw at least four pictures in a sequence and write conversation and captions to carry the story.

Prompt:
- You will work in literature circle teams and set reading goals to read *Maus and Maus II.* Some reading may be done in class and some for homework. You will have 7 days (Monday-Monday) to complete this reading.
- Discuss the questions below in your teams:
  - How does your perception change as you read more of these stories?
  - What do we learn about the author?
  - His father?
  - Their relationship?
  - Why did the author represent the Jews as mice, Germans—cats, other Poles—pigs, Americans—dogs?
  - How (what visual techniques) does the author/illustrator (use to) let you know if the story is in the present or in the past?
  - How is the story told?
- In teams, complete a character map (graphic organizer) for Artie and for his father. Agree on major events and divide so that each

student can storyboard a major event pictorially and in words. Share with class.

- Individually, write an essay that integrates these questions and ideas into a coherent piece.

Homework assignment in preparation for Day 11
(assigned no later than Day 7)

Ask a parent, guardian, or grandparent to tell you a story about when he/she was younger. He/she might tell you about a political event and how it impacted his/her life, or a story about high school, college, getting a first job, etc. This part is very flexible; you can even have someone tell you about a story told to him/her by a grandparent, cousin, etc. The goal is to find out more about your heritage. Take notes.

Day 11–13 Oral History

Student Learning Outcomes:

After reading and discussing *Maus* and *Maus II,* by Art Spiegelman, students will draw at least four pictures in a sequence and write conversation and captions to carry the story.

Prompt:

Using your notes and memories of the story told to you last week (by a parent, guardian, grandparent) begin planning your mini graphic novel by using the questions below as a guide:

1. How would you illustrate the story?
2. Would the characters be human or represented by animals, as was done in *Maus*?
3. Would you put yourself in the story or have the characters in the story tell it to you?
4. How could you use "quotes" or a character's words to communicate the story?

Complete your original graphic novel by Day 13.

Rubric:

	Exemplary	Effective	Acceptable	Unacceptable
Text	Story is exceptionally coherent with dialogue effectively and *creatively* used to support the visual message.	Story is coherent. Dialogue is effectively used to support the visual message.	Story is coherent and uses some dialogue to carry the message.	Story frames are not connected or are only loosely connected; therefore, only minimally coherent.
Images	Images are clear and creatively executed with attention to detail.	Images are clear; illustrator has obviously taken time to develop images.	Images are somewhat developed.	Images are not clear or well-developed.
Overall	Images and text are effectively and creatively working together to provide a rich mini example of a graphic novel.	Images evoke a tone and mood that support and enhance the text to provide a good mini example of a graphic novel.	Images and text are coherent and somewhat developed to provide a modest mini example of a graphic novel.	Images and text are not well developed and only loosely connected; therefore, this is a weak mini example of a graphic novel.

HOW DO I FIT WITHIN THE WORLD?: THE VOICE OF THE PRESENT

Day 14–15 *This I Believe*—Preparing to Write

Student Learning Outcomes:
- After reading sample "This I Believe" essays, students will write one and, once edited, submit it to a particular website.
- After writing a first draft (of each type of writing), students will work with partners to edit each piece using a guided editing tool.
- Given models, students will identify examples in their work of when formal grammar and language usage (vs. informal usage) can/cannot be used to convey the message/create the desired effect.

Prompt:
Conduct a web search and read examples of *This I Believe* essays online. (These are also available in a *This I Believe* published collection sold in bookstores.)

- www.thisibelieve.org/
- www.npr.org/thisibelieve/guide.html
- www.thisibelieve.org/essaywritingtips.html

With a partner, use a main idea/supporting details graphic organizer for three of the essays. Share these with another pair, forming a team of four.

WEBSITES FOR GRAPHIC ORGANIZERS

http://www.eduplace.com/graphicorganizer/
http://www.readwritethink.org/materials/storymap
http://www.readwritethink.org/lesson_images
http://www.graphicorganizers.com/tr.pdf
http://www.teacher.scholastic.com/reading/bestpractices/vocabulary/
     pdf/sr_allgo.pdf
http://www2.scholastic.com/browse/article.jsp?id=2983
http://www.jimwrightonline.com/pdfdocs/mainidea.pdf
http://www.region15.org/curriculum/CHARACTERIZATION-
     Portrait.pdf

Prompt to prepare for Lyric Circles:
Prepare for lyric circles (Day 18–19) by collecting lyrics that represent what you believe. Think of songs you really like. Do these represent the "big ideas" you believe in? Try a web search for lyrics about... (e.g., peace, social justice).

Day 16 *This I Believe*—Mind Map and Draft

Prompt:
- To review main ideas and information gathered from *This I Believe* essays found during the research on websites, teams share their six graphic organizers with the class.
- To prepare for writing your *This I Believe* essay, complete a graphic organizer—mind map.
- Then, begin draft of *This I Believe* essay. Finish for homework.

Day 17: *This I Believe*—Editing

Prompt:
- Peer edit the first and second drafts for coherence. Prepare final draft. The final draft will be edited for grammar and mechanics using a guided editing form.
- Research lyrics, if editing work and final draft is completed.

Day 18–19: Lyric Circles

Prompt:
- *This I Believe* editing will continue for part of a class period, if needed.
- Lyric Circles—share lyrics with which you identify and which you are willing to share with your team (or with the class). You can locate the lyrics online, or bring in the music with lyrics on a CD, audiotape, or iPod.
- In teams discuss
  - Which lyrics were selected
  - Why you selected these as particular lyrics with which you identify
  - The themes to the lyrics you have selected
- Use team chart from Lyric Circles on Day 3.

Rubric: **This I Believe** *Essays*

	Exemplary	Effective	Acceptable	Unacceptable
Content	Main thesis is clear and insightful; all evidence supports thesis	Main thesis is clear and evidence typically supports thesis	Main thesis is somewhat clear and evidence generally supports thesis	Main thesis is not clear and evidence is sketchy
Coherence and Organization	Ideas are well connected, logical, and use clear transitions	Ideas are connected, logical, and use appropriate transitions	Ideas are loosely connected, and may not consistently use clear transitions	Ideas are choppy, illogical, disjointed, and/or lacking transitions
Accuracy	No major or minor errors in punctuation, spelling, grammar	No major and only minimal minor errors in punctuation, spelling, grammar	No major and only a few minor errors in punctuation, spelling, grammar	Major and/or significant minor errors in punctuation, spelling, grammar
Creativity	Meets assignment requirements and displays a great deal of creativity	Meets assignment requirements and displays some level of creativity	Meets assignment requirements, but displays little or no creativity	Barely meets assignment requirements, and displays little creativity

Day 20: *This I Believe* Collections

Prompt:
    Find five classmates whose essays are either (a) very similar to yours or (b) each is unique, representing a different perspective. Put these in a booklet or catalog and write an introductory essay that clearly describes what the reader will see in these six essays (5 from classmates + yours = 6). How do they represent similar/different views?

Rubric:
    For *This I Believe* Collections, assess the students' collections using *This I Believe* Essay rubric, focusing on the introductory essay and the selection of essays that support the introductory thesis.

My Story: How I Fit in the World and What My Hopes and Aspirations Are
- Projects—one written and one creative choice
  - Written Project Choice—poem, lyrics, graphic novel, essay
  - Creative Choice—quilt (cloth, paper), mural, other visual arts, music...

  Examples:
  - A poetry collection, which should represent hopes and aspirations or may include selections compiled or written from each of the 4 themes.
  - Lyrics which may be shared as a song (not required) or as a poem with a visual.
  - The graphic novel will have graphics, but could be done as a PowerPoint, poster, a videography (or "filmstrip") project.

Rubric:

	Exemplary	Effective	Acceptable	Unacceptable
Art	Well-planned, visually/ musically creative, highly original, thought provoking, and well integrated with written component	Well planned, visually or musically creative, well connected to written component	Planned, supports and is connected to written component	Not well-planned and/or not well connected to written component, but included
Writing	Clear, concise, convincing, and creative with no major and limited grammatical/ mechanical errors	Clear, concise, and convincing with no major and limited grammatical/ mechanical errors	Clear and concise with minimal major or minor errors	Not clear or concise and/or has a number of major/minor errors that interfere with meaning
Presentation	Well-prepared and delivered, capturing the audience	Well-prepared and delivered	Prepared and delivered	Not well-prepared and/ or delivered

SUMMARY

In Chapter 2: *The Fabric of My Life*, students have explored their own identity and voice relative to four main questions: (a) Who am I?: The voice within; (b) Where do I come from?: The voice of the past; (c) How do I fit within the world?: The voice of the present; and (d) What are my hopes and aspirations?: The voice of the future. Students read *and* wrote poetry, lyrics, stories, essays, and graphic novels. As they work through the layered curriculum they learn about themselves and others, appreciating the diverse voices within the classroom.

CHAPTER 3

CHOICES THAT CHANGE OUR LIVES

Using Realistic Fiction and Nonfiction to Help Students Reflect on Difficult Decisions

INTRODUCTION

Young adults experience many new challenges physically, emotionally, socially, and intellectually. Life can change a great deal as they begin the pro-

The Perfect Norm, pages 45–70
Copyright © 2009 by Information Age Publishing
All rights of reproduction in any form reserved.

cess of separation from their parent(s), experience intense relationships with peers and significant others, and think about their futures. Unfortunately, some challenges can change their lives forever—death of friends or family, suicide, legal issues, drinking and driving, pregnancy, violence, emotional abuse, and divorce. This unit is about exploring decision-making and those choices that not only significantly impact the main character, but also create an intense ripple throughout the family, school, and/or community. There are four components:

- Fish! Philosophy™ and *Tears of a Tiger*
- Literature Circles
- *The 7 Habits of Highly Effective Teens*
- *Who Moved My Cheese?*

The unit begins with an introduction to the Fish! Philosophy™ (www.charthouse.com) which sets the tone for a positive, productive environment by focusing students on four key concepts: (a) be there, (b) choose your attitude, (c) make their day, and (d) play. "Be there" encourages students to attend to what is happening at the moment and what others are saying—essential for effective partner, team, and class discussions. "Choose your attitude" is about accepting responsibility for our attitude; we can choose to be positive and contribute a positive attitude toward others, the task, and the environment in general. "Make their day" is about doing something special for the teacher or other students that makes them feel good–in word or deed; it also makes the "doer" feel good. "Play" is about enjoying what we do or finding ways to accomplish even the most mundane tasks in a playful or fun way. Ideally, these principles become a way to interact within the classroom—even if the teacher, or a student, has to say to another student, "Choose your attitude." Of course, this should be said as a gentle reminder, not a criticism. The key concepts give a common language to interactions and shift the classroom atmosphere to one of a "team." Fish! is complementary to, but does not replace, the development of the necessary skills to successfully use cooperative learning in the classroom.

Tears of a Tiger and the literature circle books were written by Sharon Draper, the author featured in this unit, who provides students with realistic fiction to explore significant and real issues, as mentioned initially. While Ms. Draper writes books with characters and experiences to which her inner city, African-American students can relate, these stories do address teen issues across cultural groups. The books selected are sometimes read in seventh or eighth grade; however, the characters are in high school, so ninth and tenth graders are ideal target audiences, as well.

After setting the stage with the Fish! Philosophy™ for how the class will interact, I begin the unit with a "class read"—Draper's *Tears of a Tiger*—so that students can work through this book together. Why? Because the sensitive and intense issues require a teacher's guidance to help sort through the main character's emotional journey related to killing a friend in a car accident while drinking and driving. After reading *Tears of a Tiger*, students have an opportunity to choose a Draper book based on their own interest (plot and characters) and ability (varying lengths, levels of difficulty) to read in literature circles. Literature circles are "brain-friendly" and culturally responsive in that they enable students to take control over their learning as they set goals for how much to read each day, how they plan and accomplish the tasks as a cooperative team, and how they "show what they know" (present the learning to the class as teams and to the teacher as teams and, sometimes, as individuals). Instruction that utilizes teams increases active engagement, decreases anxiety, and naturally promotes a well-managed learning environment.

Although obviously a respected book for inclusion in this unit, *The 7 Habits of Highly Effective Teens,* by Sean Covey, is not a book that many teens would pick up on their own; it is a book parents buy their teens or teachers and counselors may choose to use to get students to think *critically* and *strategically.* The purpose of including it is *precisely* because it has such merit, but is not a "choice read" for most teens. Since it would be too tedious to get each student from the introduction to the end of the book, a "divide and conquer" by teams approach accomplishes the goal of exposing the students to the material and also allows students the responsibility and opportunity for leadership and creativity as they learn, prepare, and teach their peers. Again, using cooperative learning, giving students control, allowing them to apply their own experiences to the learning situation, and assessing in a variety of ways is differentiated, "brain-friendly," and culturally responsive. With increased control, choice, and engagement, classroom management issues virtually disappear; everyone is a part of the team.

The parable *Who Moved My Cheese?* provides students with a model from which they can create their own metaphorical short story and cartoon (or illustration). According to the McREL Study (Marzano, Pickering, & Pollock, 2001), *identifying similarities and differences* (which includes metaphors, similes, and analogies) has the strongest average effect size (1.61) on student achievement among the group of nine essential teaching strategies that indicate the highest levels of learning.

This unit incorporates Marzano's nine essential teaching strategies for increasing achievement (Marzano et al, 2001). These are listed below from descending order with respect to effect size; however, all have significant effect sizes. Throughout the unit plan, I point out these strategies by putting M (for *Marzano*) and the strategy number (1–9) in parentheses (e.g., M1) followed by a descriptor. Tate's "brain-friendly" teaching strategies, listed in brackets beside each of Marzano's nine strategies below, illustrate the similarities between the two strategies:

M1. Identifying similarities and differences [Tate: metaphors, analogies, and similes; graphic organizers; visuals; games; music, rhythm, rhyme and rap; storytelling; technology]
M2. Summarizing and note-taking [Tate: writing and reflecting; storytelling; technology]
M3. Reinforcing effort and providing recognition [Tate: humor and celebration; games; music, rhythm, rhyme and rap; technology]
M4. Homework and practice [Tate: work study and apprenticeship; games; movement; technology]
M5. Nonlinguistic representation [Tate: visuals, visualization; drawing & artwork; manipulatives & models; graphic organizers; fieldtrips; role-play, drama, charades, and pantomime; games; movement; technology]
M6. Cooperative learning [Tate: reciprocal teaching, cooperative learning, and peer coaching; games; movement; storytelling; technology]
M7. Setting objectives and providing feedback [Tate: games]
M8. Generating and testing hypotheses [Tate: brainstorming and discussion; project- and problem-based learning; work study and action research; storytelling; technology]
M9. Questions, cues, and advance organizers [Tate: graphic organizers; mnemonic devices; music, rhythm, rhyme and rap; movement; storytelling; technology]

It was my goal to create a unit that uses rich literature that is culturally relevant and to incorporate nonfiction "self-help" books, which might otherwise not be read, in meaningful and engaging ways. At the time I wrote this unit, I wanted to *apply* what I was reading in the Marzano's *Classroom Instruction That Works*. As such, this unit was a self-initiated challenge for professional development.

STUDENT LEARNING OUTCOMES FOR THE UNIT

Overall, students will be learning how to (a) be an effective team member, (b) appreciate different perspectives, (c) use problem-solving strategies, (d) sharpen their critical reading skills, and (e) develop critical writing skills, including organization, description, exposition, and writing for different audiences and purposes.

1. After watching a video on the Fish! Philosophy™ (www.charterhouse.com), students will generate, chart, and share ideas for how the four key concepts can be used in class and team work.
2. During reading (*Tears of a Tiger* and the self-chosen literature circle books), students will make predictions, record whether their predic-

tions were accurate (or what actually happened), and write summaries of events in a reading log..

3. While reading about others who must make tough decisions, students will identify factors leading to those decisions, as well as other possible decisions that could have been made.

4. While reading about the emotional challenges that characters must endure, students will record characteristics and emotions of the characters in their logs and/or complete a graphic organizer [see p. 41 for graphic organizer websites].

5. In addition to recording characters' actions and emotions in the reading log, students will write reflections on the impact of characters' decisions/choices on family, friends, school, and community and the influence on students' own lives.

6. Using a variety of graphic organizers (e.g., emotion map, bubble map, web, Venn diagram, fishbone), students will identify key events, characters, and emotions in the story, as well as the relationships between these story features.

7. After reading *The 7 Habits of Highly Effective Teens,* students will create alternate scenarios for making decisions, solving problems, and overcoming challenges other than the way characters may have.

8. Using team charts, graphic organizers, reading log entries and focused discussions, students will improve writing in summaries, descriptions, essays, letters, articles, brochures, and/or stories.

9. Given habits/strategies for making good choices in Covey's *7 Habits of Highly Effective Teens*, students will apply these to a variety of scenarios, both real and imagined.

10. After reading fiction and non-fiction books, students (individually and in teams, depending on specific assignment) will synthesize the book's experiences combining visual representations and words.

11. After reading *Who Moved My Cheese?*, students will create a metaphorical story and cartoon of their own.

OVERVIEW OF THE UNIT

This unit was not originally written as a layered curriculum. However, it fits neatly into a layered curriculum and accomplishes the same goal—differentiation. In Layer C, Fish! Philosophy, *Tears of a Tiger, The 7 Habits of Highly Effective Teens,* and literature circles lay a foundation through knowledge and comprehension, but with some higher-order thinking as well. Layer B takes students to the *next level* with each of these resources by having them interact with the materials and present their findings, focusing on application and analysis. Layer A includes activities in which the students choose, or are assigned, a writing task, sometimes with a visual representation and a presentation component that requires them to create and evaluate. For example, in *Who Moved My Cheese?* the students are required to evaluate the actions of the characters in this parable and synthesize by writing their own story and drawing their own cartoon. Throughout the unit, *Marzano's Essential Teaching Strategies* are indicated, for example, by (*M6: Cooperative Learning*).

Note: The numbers in parentheses on the table below indicate the day(s) in which an assessable activity occurs. Rubrics are included for each type of assessment—written, visual, chart/presentation. Reading logs are used formatively to determine whether or not a student is reading and comprehending the text.

Components	Layer C	Layer B	Layer A
Fish! and *Tears of a Tiger*	Create and share Team Chart—Fish! (1) Write in reading log (2–4)	Complete visual representations— web, emotion map, fishbone organizer (3, 4–6) Write a description (3)	Choice: write letters, or essays, or create booklets or a visual representation w/ an executive summary (7–8) Present choice (9–10)
Literature circles	Create and share team posters (18–20) Write in reading log (12–17)	Create and share team Foldables® (18–20)	Write an individual essay (18–21)
The 7 Habits of Highly Effective Teens	Create a 7-flap Foldable® on *7 Habits* (28–30) Write in reading logs (22–24)	Create and present Team chart presentations— principles (23, 24, 31) Create and share Team Habit Presentation (28–30)	Write an individual essay relating a "habit" to a literature circle book (31–33) Create a visual representation related to essay (34–35)
Who Moved My Cheese?			Create either an essay or a cartoon (39–40)

Note: This unit was written as directions for teachers, as opposed to the *Fabric of My Life* unit. So, the prompts are written for teachers while the assignemnts and rubrics are written for students.

FISH! PHILOSOPHY AND TEARS OF A TIGER

Day 1: Fish!

Watch Fish! DVD so students learn key Fish! Philosophy concepts—(a) choose their attitude, (b) be there, (c) make their day, and (d) play—as a prelude to participating fully in class and in teams. (M5: nonlinguistic representation) Discuss observations from the DVD after viewing, leading students to identify the four concepts and relate them to how we function in our class. Generate and chart ideas on how we could use these when we work in small groups or as a whole class. (M8: generating and testing hypotheses) Explain to students that we will use these concepts/practices as we move into the literature segment of the unit—*Choices That Change Our Lives.*

FISH! Team Chart and Presentation Rubric

	Exemplary (4)	Effective (3)	Acceptable (2)	Unacceptable (1)
Content	All four concepts are clear and at least three insightful ideas are included for each concept	All four concepts are clear with at least two ideas included for each concept	The four concepts are somewhat clear with at least one idea included for each concept	The four concepts are not clear and/or only vague ideas are included for some or all of the concepts
Presentation— coherence and organization	Ideas are well connected, logical, and use clear transitions and are delivered in a clear articulate manner	Ideas are connected, logical, and use appropriate transitions and are delivered in an articulate manner	Ideas are loosely connected, and may not consistently use clear transitions and are delivered in a reasonably articulate manner	Ideas are choppy, illogical, disjointed, and/or lacking transitions and are not delivered in an articulate manner
Correctness	No major or minor errors in punctuation, spelling, grammar	No major and only minimal minor errors in punctuation, spelling, grammar	No major and only a few minor errors in punctuation, spelling, grammar	Major and/ or significant minor errors in punctuation, spelling, grammar
Creativity	Meets assignment requirements and displays a great deal of creativity	Meets assignment requirements and displays some level of creativity	Meets assignment requirements, but displays little or no creativity	Barely meets assignment requirements, and displays little creativity
Team effort	Each team member is focused, contributing to and learning from the team activity	Each team member is focused, contributing some and learning from the team activity	Most team members are focused and trying to engage all members in contributing to and learning from the activity	Not all team members are focused, contributing, or learning, or only one or two members are completing the assignment

Scoring: Add up points earned _____ divide by 5 = _____ Final score

Day 2: *Tears of a Tiger*

Introduce the author and the types of books she writes. Sharon M. Draper has taught high school English/language arts for twenty-five years in Cincinnati, Ohio. In 1997, Ms. Draper was *National Teacher of the Year.* She was one of the first Nationally Board Certified English/language arts teachers in the country and serves on the Board of Directors of the National Board for Professional Teaching Standards. She has written many poems, essays, short stories, and books. She has won the Coretta Scott King Award for three of her books. Ms. Draper has been a speaker internationally. *Tears of A Tiger* was Ms. Draper's first novel, one of her award-winning books.

Note: The following are notes to the teacher on what to highlight for students each day within the unit of study. Reading assignments may appear long, but this book is a very quick read. Many chapters are one—two pages and include poems, news articles, and narratives. Vocabulary will be identified by students or the teacher during reading, and recorded in reading logs for class discussion:

- Read the opening page that describes the accident. Ask students to identify what they think is happening in this scene/what is not said/ and what they predict will be the outcome (the boys were drinking and driving, they hit a wall, one dies). (M8—generate hypothesis)
- Have students read the newspaper article silently (pages 1–2). How does this confirm or change what you thought was happening? What details did you find out that you did not predict? (M8—test hypothesis). How do you feel about this situation?
- Begin reading log, which will include notes, summarizing statements, and any personal feelings or reflections. This log may include drawings to enhance the representation of the students' perceptions and feelings. This log will be kept daily for homework, although students should bring it to class for discussions and add notes from in-class readings. The teacher will keep a checklist (see below).

Reading Log Checklist							
Includes:	Ch 1	Ch 2	Ch 3	. . .			
hypothesis							
summaries							
notes							
perceptions							
feelings							
vocabulary							

- On page 3, note the date of this chapter. What do you think this will be about? (M8: generating and testing hypotheses) After reading this chapter, write a brief summary (M2: summarizing and note taking) about whether or not your hypotheses were correct and/ or what information supported or changed your hypotheses (M8: generating and testing hypotheses).
- Read pages 3–19. In the reading log, list characters and notes about characters. (M2: summarizing and note taking; M 4: homework and practice)

Day 3

Remind class of the four Fish! philosophy principles and ask how these will be important when we move into teams. In teams of four (M6: cooperative learning), identify the characters introduced in the first five short chapters using a web (M5: graphic organizer, M2: summarizing and note taking) that shows who each is and how each relates to the others (e.g., Tyrone—basketball player, in car, fell out, helped Andy out of driver's seat—connected to Andy [basketball team, in car accident], Robert- longtime friend, Rhonda—girlfriend). Characters to include at this point—Robert, Andy, BJ, Tyrone, Keisha, Rhonda, (Gerald and police officer may be included by students). Share with class and look for similarities and differences (M1: identifying similarities and differences).

As a whole class, look at *The Hazelwood Herald* (pages 21–23), have students volunteer to read small articles in the school paper aloud. Use these questions as advance organizers (M9: questions, cues, and advance organizers): What themes do you see in the articles? What is the tone of the newspaper? How do you know?

On pages 23–29, Andy has a conversation with the coach. Get two students to read—one as Andy and one as Coach. Students will listen in order to describe how Andy feels and what his concerns are at this point in the story. Each student will divide a piece of paper in half to create two columns. They will be given a few minutes at the end of the reading to list topics/concerns Andy discussed with the coach in the left hand column and Andy's feelings in the right hand column in their reading logs. (M2: summarizing and note taking)

[As a class, have students provide specific examples of how they are using the Fish! principles—be there, choose your attitude, make their day, and play—in their team work.] (M3: reinforcing effort and providing recognition)

Read pages 30–51 (finish for homework as necessary). What do we learn from Rhonda's letter and from Gerald's English assignment? How do they feel toward Andy? What do we know about how Andy is doing from Rhonda's and Gerald's writings? In the chapter "Hoops and Dunks," how does Andy seem? What do we learn about Andy in "How Do I Feel?" Describe the interaction between Keisha and Andy in "Girl Problems?" (M9: questions, cues, and advance organizers; M4: homework and practice)

Description Rubric

	Exemplary (4)	Effective (3)	Acceptable (2)	Unacceptable (1)
Accuracy	All statements are clear and accurate with respect to the situation/ content	Most statements are clear and accurate	Most/many statements are reasonably clear and accurate	Few statements are clear and/ or accurate
Coherence	Ideas are well connected, logical, and use clear transitions	Ideas are connected, logical, and use appropriate transitions	Ideas are loosely connected, and may not consistently use clear transitions	Ideas are choppy, illogical, disjointed, and/or lacking transitions
Correctness	No major or minor errors in punctuation, spelling, grammar	No major and only minimal minor errors in punctuation, spelling, grammar	No major and only a few minor errors in punctuation, spelling, grammar	Major and/ or significant minor errors in punctuation, spelling, grammar

Scoring: Add up points earned _____ divide by 3 = _____ Final score

Day 4

Create an emotion map linked with events in the story—like a fishbone graphic organizer (e.g., initial feelings when accident occurs—shock; when Andy returns to school—feelings expressed in conversation with coach; the big game—sadness; Andy's first visit to the psychologist— guilt). (M5: nonlinguistic representations)

Read pages 52–70; add to the fishbone.

Read pages to 71–88; take notes in reading log, and write a summarizing statement (1–2 sentences) for each chapter. (M2: summarizing and note taking; M4: homework and practice; M7: setting objectives and providing feedback)

Day 5

In literature circles, discuss purpose of last night's reading and add to fishbone.

Predict what will happen next; read pages 89–113. Discuss and add to fishbone.

Read pages 114–135; take notes in reading log, and write a summarizing statement (1–2 sentences) for each chapter. (M2: summarizing and note taking; M4: homework and practice; M5: nonlinguistic representations; M6: cooperative learning; M7: setting objectives and providing feedbacks; M8: generating and testing hypotheses)

Finish for homework, if necessary.

[As a class, have students provide specific examples of how they are using the Fish! principles—be there, choose your attitude, make their day, and play—in their team work.] (M3: reinforcing effort and providing recognition)

Day 6

In literature circles, discuss purpose of weekend reading and add to fishbone. Read pages 136–162; take notes in reading log, and write a summarizing statement (1–2 sentences) for each chapter. (M2: summarizing and note taking; M4: homework and practice)

Predict what will happen next; read chapters pages 163–180. Discuss and complete fishbone. (M2: summarizing and note taking; M3: reinforcing effort and providing recognition; M5: nonlinguistic representations; M6: cooperative learning; M8: generating and testing hypotheses)

[As a class, have students provide specific examples of how they are using the Fish! principles—be there, choose your attitude, make their day, and play—in their team work.] (M3: reinforcing effort and providing recognition)

Days 7–8

Assessment: Reading logs; observations of team work, and fishbone/ web graphic organizers; writing options (see below). (Draft on Wednesday, polish on Thursday with feedback from teacher.) (M7: setting objectives and providing feedback)

Choice Assignment:

Note: Allowing student choice in what they produce is a brain-friendly strategy and a culturally relevant teaching strategy. Choice creates novelty, which results in engagement and supports a well-managed classroom of students focused on a task rather than off-task behavior.

- Write a letter to Andy, his parents, the psychologist, or any other character in the book, expressing how you feel and what you think. (Letter Rubric below.)
- Write a letter to another (real) friend who is experiencing problems. (Letter Rubric below.)
- Write about a time when you had a problem and what strategies you tried to resolve the problem. (Essay Rubric below.)
- Make a booklet/brochure about drinking and driving; depression and/or suicide, or some other issue for your age group. Students should get approval for the topic prior to making the booklet or brochure. (Rubric for Evaluating Booklet... below.)
- Draw a visual representation for the book and describe this visual representation in an "executive summary" of what the visual represents. (Rubric for Evaluating Booklet... below.)

Letter Rubric

	Exemplary (4)	Effective (3)	Acceptable (2)	Unacceptable (1)
Purpose	Clear and insightful	Clear	Somewhat clear	Not clear
Tone	Personal, fair-minded, thoughtful	Personal and reasonably fair-minded	Somewhat personal and reasonably fair-minded	Either not personal or not fair-minded
Format (address, date, greeting, body, salutation)	Uses all components of a letter in correct form	Uses all/ most of the components of a letter in reasonably correct form— date, greeting, body, salutation	Uses some components of a letter in a somewhat correct form— greeting, body, and salutation	May use few or no components and/or components are not in order, which impedes the reader's understanding
Accuracy	All statements are clear and accurate with respect to the situation/ content	Most statements are clear and accurate	Most/many statements are reasonably clear and accurate	Few statements are clear and/ or accurate

Coherence	Ideas are well connected, logical, and use clear transitions	Ideas are connected, logical, and use appropriate transitions	Ideas are loosely connected, and may not consistently use clear transitions	Ideas are choppy, illogical, disjointed, and/or lacking transitions
Correctness	No major or minor errors in punctuation, spelling, grammar	No major and only minimal minor errors in punctuation, spelling, grammar	No major and only a few minor errors in punctuation, spelling, grammar	Major and/or significant minor errors in punctuation, spelling, grammar
Creativity	Meets assignment requirements and displays a great deal of creativity	Meets assignment requirements and displays some level of creativity	Meets assignment requirements, but displays little or no creativity	Barely meets assignment requirements, and displays little creativity

Scoring: Add up points earned _____ divide by 7 = _____ Final score

Essay Rubric

	Exemplary (4)	Effective (3)	Acceptable (2)	Unacceptable (1)
Content	Main thesis is clear and insightful; all evidence supports thesis	Main thesis is clear and evidence typically supports thesis	Main thesis is somewhat clear and evidence generally supports thesis	Main thesis is not clear and evidence is sketchy
Coherence and Organization	Ideas are well connected, logical, and use clear transitions	Ideas are connected, logical, and use appropriate transitions	Ideas are loosely connected, and may not consistently use clear transitions	Ideas are choppy, illogical, disjointed, and/or lacking transitions
Correctness	No major or minor errors in punctuation, spelling, grammar	No major and only minimal minor errors in punctuation, spelling, grammar	No major and only a few minor errors in punctuation, spelling, grammar	Major and/or significant minor errors in punctuation, spelling, grammar
Creativity	Meets assignment requirements and displays a great deal of creativity	Meets assignment requirements and displays some level of creativity	Meets assignment requirements, but displays little or no creativity	Barely meets assignment requirements, and displays little creativity

Scoring: Add up points earned _____ divide by 4 = _____ Final score

Rubric for Evaluating Booklet, Catalog, Brochure, Posters,
or Visual Representation with Executive Summary

	Exemplary	Effective	Acceptable	Unacceptable
Art	Well-planned, visually/ musically creative, highly original, thought provoking, and well integrated with written component	Well planned, visually or musically creative, well connected to written component	Planned, supports and is connected to written component	Not well-planned and/or not well connected to written component, but includes some art
Writing	Clear, concise, convincing, and creative with no major and limited grammatical/ mechanical errors	Clear, concise, and convincing with no major and limited grammatical/ mechanical errors	Clear and concise with minimal major or minor errors	Not clear or concise and/or has a number of major/minor errors that interfere with meaning
Presentation	Well-prepared and delivered, highly articulate, capturing the audience	Well-prepared and articulately delivered	Prepared and delivered somewhat articulately	Not well-prepared and/ or delivered articulately

Scoring: Add up points earned _____ divide by 3 = _____ Final score

Days 9–10

Share letters, essays, booklets, visual representations with class.

[As a class, have students provide specific examples of how they are using the Fish! Philosophy principles—be there, choose your attitude, make their day, and play—in their team work.] (M3: reinforcing effort and providing recognition)

LITERATURE CIRCLES

(M4: homework and practice; M6: cooperative learning)

Day 11

Present some very brief book talks on other Sharon Draper books to acquaint students with the books from which they will select and read in literature circles (limit five students per group, although some groups may have the same book). Differentiation is provided in two ways: (a) books vary in length (allowing readers to select a manageable length book for their speed and overall reading ability, and (b) some books are on tape (for those who may need some assistance with reading). Students will meet in literature circles to make a plan for reading the book. This plan includes an agreement of how many pages per day (e.g., in class and homework/ eight days, including weekend/approximately thirty pages a day) they need to agree to accomplish; a system for assigning and rotating lit circle roles (e.g., discussion director, summarizer, vocabulary finder, question writer, story mapper); and a discussion which generates a hypotheses, based on the book talks and having the book in hand.

Days 12–17

Students will chart generated hypotheses and confirm/change for each chapter as they are reading through their book as a way to set purposes for reading (generate and test hypotheses) and keep notes on their novel in a reading log. (This log includes all hypotheses, notes, summaries, and personal reactions.) Vocabulary will be identified by students during reading and recorded in reading logs for team discussion. Students should identify at least two words for study from daily reading.

As a team, they will also do a web for characters and a fishbone of events and emotions. (M2: summarizing and note taking; M5: nonlinguistic representations; M6: cooperative learning; M8: generating and testing hypotheses)

[Daily, as a class, have students provide specific examples of how they are using the Fish! principles—be there, choose your attitude, make their day, and play—in their team work.] (M3: reinforcing effort and providing recognition)

Days 18–20

Assessment:

1. As a team, design a poster about your book. Include character maps, plot flow maps, your reactions to five events, and pictures about significant events in the story. Use Poster and Presentation Rubric (below).

Poster and Presentation Rubric

	Exemplary (4)	Effective (3)	Acceptable (2)	Unacceptable (1)
Content	Includes clear and insightful reactions about 5 events, and complete and detailed character and plot maps	Includes clear reactions about 4–5 events, and complete and fairly detailed character and plot maps	Includes clear reactions for at least 3 events, and includes character and plot maps	Reactions are not clear and/or only 2 or fewer events are included; character and plot maps are vague, sketchy or missing
Presentation: Coherence and Organization	Ideas are well connected, logical, and use clear transitions and are delivered in a clear articulate manner	Ideas are connected, logical, and use appropriate transitions and are delivered in an articulate manner	Ideas are loosely connected, and may not consistently use clear transitions and are delivered in a reasonably articulate manner	Ideas are choppy, illogical, disjointed, and/or lacking transitions and is not delivered in an articulate manners
Correctness	No major or minor errors in punctuation, spelling, grammar	No major and only minimal minor errors in punctuation, spelling, grammar	No major and only a few minor errors in punctuation, spelling, grammar	Major and/or significant minor errors in punctuation, spelling, grammar
Creativity	Meets assignment requirements and displays a great deal of creativity	Meets assignment requirements and displays some level of creativity	Meets assignment requirements, but displays little or no creativity	Barely meets assignment requirements, and displays little creativity
Team Effort	Each team member is focused, contributing to and learning from the team activity	Each team member is focused, contributing some and learning from the team activity	Most team members are focused and trying to engage all members in contributing to and learning from the activity	Not all team members are focused, contributing, or learning, Or one or two members are completing the assignment

Scoring: Add up points earned _____ divide by 5 = _____ Final score

2. Compare aspects of your novel with *Tears of A Tiger*—first drawing (or using a three-tab Foldable® to create) a bubble map/Venn diagram as a team (formative assessment). [To make a three-tab Fold-

able®, fold paper in half, hot dog style, then fold into thirds and cut along short folds to center fold on one side.]

3. Then, individually, write an essay (minimum of five paragraphs—introduction, brief summary of each book, including similarities, differences, and conclusion). Use Essay Rubric from Days 7–8. (M1: identifying similarities and differences; M2: summarizing and note taking; M5: nonlinguistic representations; M6: cooperative learning)

[As a class, have students provide specific examples of how they are using the Fish! principles—*be there, choose your attitude, make their day, and play*—in their team work.] (M3: reinforcing effort and providing recognition)

Day 21

Share team posters. Evaluate with Poster and Presentation Rubric from Days 18–20.

Submit essays. Evaluate with Essay Rubric from Days 7–8.

THE 7 HABITS OF HIGHLY EFFECTIVE TEENS

Day 22

Open with the riddle in *The 7 Habits of Highly Effective Teens*: What Am I? (A habit). We have been reading about some very difficult issues that teens have to face. Today, we will begin Part III of our unit, which will focus on strategies or "habits" that effective teens strive for on a daily basis, so that whether the challenges are more serious, or less serious, you have some tools to fortify you. Read aloud the first chapter to class, showing displays (overhead or digital projection) of (a) 7 habits of highly effective teens (p. 5); (b) tree of how habits build on each other (from p. 6) (M5: non-linguistic representations); and (c) 7 habits of highly *defective* teens (p. 7). (M 5: nonlinguistic representations; M7: setting objectives and providing feedback)

Read *Paradigms and Principles* aloud or have students volunteer to read one of the *Top 10 All-Time Stupid Quotes* and eight common statements made by real teens (pages 11–12). Read pages 13–28 to define paradigm and identify the factors that influence our paradigms of ourselves and others. What is principle-centered? Why does Covey recommend "baby steps?" Keep notes in reading log. Summarize main points at the end of each chapter. (Finish for homework, if necessary, and be ready to discuss in teams on Day 23). Form 5–6 teams for Days 23–24: (M2: summarizing and note-taking; M4: homework and practice)

Day 23

Teams meet, discuss paradigms and principles, and chart key points to share with whole class. Each team reports, then the class looks for *similarities/differences* across the charts and comes to consensus about a class definition and key points. (M1: identifying similarities and differences; M6: cooperative learning)

Begin *The Personal Bank Account* (pages 31–46) by reading the poem on page 33 (about change beginning with self). On pages 45–46, complete and record responses for twelve tasks/questions to respond to (e.g., Keep Promises to Yourself, Do Random Acts of Service, Tap Into Your Talents). Finish for homework, if necessary, and be ready to discuss in teams on Day 24. (M1: identifying similarities and differences; M4: homework and practice)

[As a class, have students provide specific examples of how they are using the Fish! principles—*be there, choose your attitude, make their day, and play*—in their team work.] (M3: reinforcing effort and providing recognition)

Day 24

In teams, discuss the main headings of the tasks/questions (Keep Promises to Yourself, etc.), students giving personal examples or non-personal examples based on their comfort level. Each team discusses charted key points/examples from this chapter with the whole class. Tomorrow, we will begin focused work on the habits of highly effective teens. (M6: cooperative learning; M7: setting objectives and providing feedback)

Team Chart and Presentation Rubric

	Exemplary (4)	Effective (3)	Acceptable (2)	Unacceptable (1)
Content	Includes clear, accurate, and insightful ideas	Includes clear and accurate ideas	Includes reasonably clear and accurate ideas	Ideas are not clear and/or not accurate
Presentation: coherence and organization	Ideas are well connected, logical, and use clear transitions and are delivered in a clear articulate manner	Ideas are connected, logical, and use appropriate transitions and are delivered in an articulate manner	Ideas are loosely connected, and may not consistently use clear transitions and are delivered in a reasonably articulate manner	Ideas are choppy, illogical, disjointed, and/or lacking transitions and are not delivered in an articulate manner
Correctness	No major or minor errors in punctuation, spelling, grammar	No major and only minimal minor errors in punctuation, spelling, grammar	No major and only a few minor errors in punctuation, spelling, grammar	Major and/or significant minor errors in punctuation, spelling, grammar
Creativity	Meets assignment requirements and displays a great deal of creativity	Meets assignment requirements and displays some level of creativity	Meets assignment requirements, but displays little or no creativity	Barely meets assignment requirements, and displays little creativity
Team effort	Each team member is focused, contributing to and learning from the team activity	Each team member is focused, contributing some and learning from the team activity	Most team members are focused and trying to engage all members in contributing to and learning from the activity	Not all team members are focused, contributing, or learning, or only one or two members are completing the assignment

Scoring: Add up points earned _____ divide by 5 = _____ Final score

Days 25–27

Divide into seven new teams and have each team read one of the chapters on a habit and prepare a presentation (e.g., poster, PowerPoint, skit with summarizing handout) to teach the other groups about their "effective habit." (M2: summarizing and note taking; M5: nonlinguistic representations; M6: cooperative learning; M7: setting objectives and providing feedback)

[As a class, have students provide specific examples of how they are using the Fish! principles—*be there, choose your attitude, make their day, and play*—in their team work.] (M3: reinforcing effort and providing recognition)

Days 28–30

Teams will share their "habit" presentations (2–3 per day). Use Team Chart and Presentation Rubric from Day 24.

Each student will complete a seven-flap Foldable® on the 7 Habits, demonstrating what they learned from the Habit presentations. (M1: identifying similarities and differences; M5: nonlinguistic representations; M6: cooperative learning)

7-Flap Foldable® Rubric

	Exemplary (4)	Effective (3)	Acceptable (2)	Unacceptable (1)
Content	Includes complete, detailed, clear, and accurate information on all 7 Habits from the presentations	Includes complete, clear, and accurate information on at least 5 Habits and some information on all 7 Habits	Includes reasonably clear and accurate information on at least 4 Habits and some information on at least 6 Habits	Includes some information, but it is not complete, clear and/or accurate; does not show an acceptable level of mastery.

[As a class, have students provide specific examples of how they are using the Fish! principles—*be there, choose your attitude, make their day, and play*—in their team work.] (M3: reinforcing effort and providing recognition)

Day 31

Students will get in their literature circles from PART II and use the 7 Habits to rethink how their main character's life might have been different if he/she had used the 7 Habits (all or some).

Chart ideas as a team (formative assessment activity). Individuals choose one of the ideas to explore in an essay.

Use Essay Rubric from Days 7–8. (M1: identifying similarities and differences; M2: summarizing and note taking; M3: reinforcing effort and providing recognition; M4: homework and practice; M6: cooperative learning; M8: generating and testing hypotheses)

Day 32

In teams, conduct peer review and editing of essays for clarity, coherence, and grammatical and mechanical errors.

Use class time and home time to complete final, polished copy to submit on Day 33. (M3: reinforcing effort and providing recognition; M6: cooperative learning; M7: setting objectives and providing feedback)

Peers should also evaluate with the Essay Rubric from Days 7–8. However, a checklist may be helpful in ensuring the Peer Review and Editing includes a review of basic grammar and mechanics within the essay.

PEER REVIEW AND EDITING CHECKLIST

Check each item below after you have edited the writing for each feature.

SENTENCES
- Subject/verb agreement _____
- Appropriate and consistent tense _____
- No sentence fragments _____
- Recommended: active voice whenever possible _____

CAPITAL LETTERS
- First word in each sentence is capitalized _____
- Titles of books and movies _____
- Titles of persons _____
- Proper nouns _____

PUNCTUATION
- Each sentence has appropriate end punctuation _____
- Commas appear to be used correctly _____
- Apostrophes are used correctly _____
- Quotation marks are used correctly _____

COMMENTS:

Day 33

Submit the polished essay. Teacher will evaluate with the Essay Rubric from Days 7–8.

In the 7 Habits teams, discuss how the three parts of this unit are linked together (I—Fish! and *Tears of a Tiger*; II—Literature Circle Books; and III—*The 7 Habits of Highly Effective Teens*).

Create a visual representation of the relationship (bubble map, Venn Diagram, other). (M5: nonlinguistic representations; M6: cooperative learning)

Days 34–35

Share visual representations. (M5: nonlinguistic representations; M6: cooperative learning)

Use the Rubric for Evaluating Booklet, Catalog, Brochure, Posters, or Visual Representation with Executive Summary.

Part III Assessment (described): (a) team presentation; (b) seven-flap Foldable® (individual); and (c) individual essay relating a habit to a literature circle book.

Who Moved My Cheese?

Day 36–38

This 94-page parable will be read aloud to the class. While listening, students can draw sketches of the scenes and interactions. At the end of each chapter, there is a statement that will provide the impetus for discussion (e.g., "Movement in a New Direction Helps You Find New Cheese"). What does this mean? How did the characters come to this conclusion? A full reading and discussion will take about three days. (M5: nonlinguistic representations)

Day 39

Write an essay or develop a cartoon about a situation in which you were faced with change. Describe the circumstances. How did you feel? What did you do? Would you do anything different in retrospect? (M5: nonlinguistic representations)

Evaluate essay with Essay Rubric from Days 7–8.

Day 40

View the *Who Moved My Cheese* video (15 minutes).
Have students share essays or cartoons.
Assessment: Essay or Cartoon Rubric

Essay Rubric

	Exemplary	Effective	Acceptable	Unacceptable
Content	Main thesis is clear and insightful; all evidence supports thesis	Main thesis is clear and evidence typically supports thesis	Main thesis is somewhat clear and evidence generally supports thesis	Main thesis is not clear and evidence is sketchy
Coherence and Organization	Ideas are well connected, logical, and use clear transitions	Ideas are connected, logical, and use appropriate transitions	Ideas are loosely connected, and may not consistently use clear transitions	Ideas are choppy, illogical, disjointed, and/or lacking transitions
Accuracy	No major or minor errors in punctuation, spelling, grammar	No major and only minimal minor errors in punctuation, spelling, grammar	No major and only a few minor errors in punctuation, spelling, grammar	Major and/ or significant minor errors in punctuation, spelling, grammar
Creativity	Meets assignment requirements and displays a great deal of creativity	Meets assignment requirements and displays some level of creativity	Meets assignment requirements, but displays little or no creativity	Barely meets assignment requirements, and displays little creativity

Cartoon Rubric

	Exemplary	Effective	Acceptable	Unacceptable
Text	Story is exceptionally coherent with dialogue effectively and creatively used to support the visual message.	Story is coherent. Dialogue is effectively used to support the visual message.	Story is coherent and uses some dialogue to carry the message.	Story frames are not connected or are only loosely connected; therefore, only minimally coherent.
Images	Images are clear and creatively executed with attention to detail.	Images are clear; illustrator has obviously taken time to develop images.	Images are somewhat developed.	Images are not clear or well-developed.
Overall	Images and text are effectively and creatively working together to provide a rich cartoon.	Images evoke a tone and mood that support and enhance the text to provide a good cartoon.	Images and text are coherent and somewhat developed to provide a modest cartoon.	Images and text are not well developed and only loosely connected; therefore, this is a weak cartoon.

UNIT EXTENSIONS

Note: For continued studies, students could research one of the issues (e.g., drug abuse, depression, child abuse) and develop a poster to help peers know more about what the issue is and how to get help.

SUMMARY

In Chapter 3: *Choices That Change Our Lives,* students reflected on difficult decisions that adolescents and young adults face. They read both fiction and nonfiction, engaged in literature circles, worked in teams, and taught each other. Students felt the struggles and, sometimes, tragedies they read about throughout the realistic fiction choices. They also thought through issues from a more intellectual problem-solving and decision-making, rather than emotional, perspective using non-fiction "self-help" books. Using a layered curriculum, students used reading, writing, and visual literacy to make sense of their world.

MATERIALS/BOOKS USED OR REFERENCED IN THIS UNIT

Tears of a Tiger

Andy Jackson and his friends were celebrating their basketball victory with a few beers. When Andy drives into a retaining wall and the car catches on fire, one of his friends is trapped in the car and dies. The entire student body at Hazelwood High is stunned; however, Andy struggles with the loss of his friend and team member the most since he was driving the car. This is a story about how Andy comes to terms with the accident, the loss of his friend, and his role in it.

Descriptions for Sharon Draper's other books can be accessed at www. sharondraper.com.

The 7 Habits of Highly Effective Teens

This book is about seven habits that will improve the life of teens (and everyone really). These habits are contrasted with seven habits of highly defective teens. The author discusses having a balanced life and about shifting paradigms to be highly effective and happy.

Who Moved My Cheese? (book and video)

This allegorical story is cute. There are two mice—Scurry and Scout—and two little men—Hem and Haw. They each approach the world (their maze) differently and the reader sees how the decisions they make impact their ability to change when things change around them.

BOOKS, DVDS, AND OTHER LITERATURE LIST

Whole Class Viewing and Reading

- *Tears of a Tiger*. Sharon M. Draper. New York: Simon & Schuster. 1994. (183 pages) ISBN: 0–689–31878–2. [This book is a part of the Hazelwood High School Trilogy.]
- Fish! DVD (for schools)

Literature Circle Suggestions
(also by Sharon M. Draper)

- *Forged by Fire*. Sharon M. Draper. New York: Simon & Schuster. 1997. (151 pages) ISBN: 0–689–80699-X. [This book is a part of the Hazelwood High School Trilogy.]
- *Darkness Before Dawn*. Sharon M. Draper. New York: Simon & Schuster. 2001. (233 pages) ISBN: 0–689–83080–7 [This book is a part of the Hazelwood High School Trilogy.]
- *Double Dutch*. Sharon M. Draper. New York: Simon & Schuster. 2001. (183 pages) ISBN: 0–689–84230–9.
- *The Battle of Jericho*. Sharon M. Draper. New York: Simon & Schuster. 2003. (297 pages) ISBN: 0–689–84232–5.
- *We Beat the Street*. Sharon M. Draper. New York: Dutton. 2005. (194 pages) ISBN: 0–525–47407–2.
- *Romiette and Julio*. Sharon M. Draper. New York: Simon & Schuster. 1999. (236 pages) ISBN: 0–689–82180–8

Other Books/Literature

- *The 7 Habits of Highly Effective Teens*. Sean Covey. New York: Franklin Covey Co. 1998. (244 pages) ISBN: 0–7432–5815–0.
- *Who Moved My Cheese for Teens*. Spencer Johnson, M.D. New York: G. P. Putnam's Sons. 2002. (94 pages) ISBN: 0–399–24007–1.
- Agency pamphlets and Internet research on social issues

For Teachers

- *Teaching from the Heart*. Sharon M. Draper. New York: Heinemann Books. 1999. ISBN 0–325–00131–6.
- *Not Quite Burned Out But Crispy Around the Edges*. Sharon M. Draper. New York: Heinemann Books. 2001. ISBN: 0–325–00365–3.
- *Classroom Instruction That Works*. Robert J. Marzano, Debra J. Pickering, and Jane E. Pollock VA.: ASCD. 2001. ISBN: 0–87120–504–1.

CHAPTER 4

COMMUNITY AND CULTURE

Understanding Ourselves and Others in the Global Community

INTRODUCTION

More than at any other time, we are faced with the realization that we live in a global community. Thus, significant twenty-first century goals for schools include both a global focus and international understanding. With that in mind, we must be committed to empowering students not only to being successful in school, but also to expanding their knowledge of themselves,

The Perfect Norm, pages 71–96
Copyright © 2009 by Information Age Publishing
All rights of reproduction in any form reserved.

their community, and other communities and cultures. Unlike *The Fabric of My Life* unit in which students focus more on themselves—past, present and future—this *Community and Culture* unit focuses on the world, the part of it in which they live and the parts they need to understand to function in an ever-changing, sometimes "flat" world (Friedman, 2005).

Historical, cultural, and social treasures are often hidden in plain sight in our communities. We take our "place" for granted, perhaps knowing of some historical places, but not truly understanding their significance. Yet, when we go to another community or country, those are just the places we seek. It is our belief that we must understand who we are and what our "place" is all about before we can truly interpret similarities and differences among other places. Of course, with rising gas prices and school system regulations, students cannot always go on extensive field trips. In this unit, teachers create stations that serve as a mock multi-site fieldtrip of Durham. Additionally, these teacher-developed stations serve as models for how students might approach developing their stations for the countries they are assigned. This unit focuses on strategies such as field trips, visuals, reciprocal teaching and cooperative learning, and models—all "brain-friendly" strategies. Learning about one's community is also, as you may have surmised, culturally sensitive if appropriately planned and inclusive.

Interestingly, Durham, North Carolina was once called Durham Station. It has a rich, multi-faceted history. Durham's history has been significant in its relationship to the growth of the tobacco industry and in its conversion to being part of the Research Triangle, a high tech, science-savvy environment. Durham has a history which includes slavery on nearby plantations and a successful "Black Wall Street" prior to desegregation. Black leaders and visionaries have exhibited a strong presence over many years and have worked hand-in-hand with well-known White leaders. Albeit in parallel societies initially, historical documents clearly show supportive relationships across racial lines in times when this was not considered "acceptable." Durham has two well-known universities: North Carolina Central University is the first historically black *liberal arts* university in the nation. Duke University is a small, private institution which has been linked in many ways to the Dukes of Durham, whose philanthropy helped Duke University to thrive during the early years of its existence. There is so much to Durham, as there is to anyone's "place." However, Durham is our "place," so we proudly use it as a model for this unit.

Today's world requires students to have a more global, international perspective. While this begins with a strong knowledge base, it also requires opportunities to interact with and understand others. In this unit, these interactions are threefold. First, the students interact with a variety of teachers, some of whom may be implementing newly acquired knowledge and strategies as they engage in research, modeling, and facilitation, rather than just dispensing textbook knowledge. Second, the students interact with each other on teams that plan, learn, research, and create together and share what they've learned with other students in a multi-cultural culminating event. By working together in teams, they learn more about each other as well as different perspectives on the content and approaches to the tasks. If implemented at the beginning of the middle school experience or as a summer bridge experience between elementary and middle school, students can meet new students from other feeder elementary schools, another benefit of this pedagogy. Third, the students interact with contacts they use while researching, as well as guest speakers from various cultures and countries, gaining first-hand experience and information from others who are knowledgeable about, have lived in, or are from those countries.

The unit theme is also significant because it helps prepare students for success in middle school social studies; as such they will have a "leg up" on the curriculum content for all three middle grade levels. Middle school students study South America, Europe, and Russia in sixth grade; Africa, Asia, and Australia in seventh grade; and North Carolina in the eighth grade. This part of the unit, in which teams research and share different countries in some way, has been implemented in some form by other teachers. It is the initial component of "place-based" learning about Durham and the modeling of process that makes this unit unique. If used at the end of the middle school experience when students study North Carolina History in the eighth grade, the components could be reversed. The students could still create the "country" stations, building on what they learned in sixth and seventh grade social studies. Then, they could research and prepare the Durham stations.

This unit requires students to expand their communication, literacy, research, and technology skills. Students work in teams to discuss and prepare visual and written presentations using available technologies. They present what they have learned, supported by visual aids they have created, with other teams in a multi-cultural culminating event at the end of the unit. In so doing, each student has an opportunity to contribute to a major project based on his/her strengths within the team. Students become the "teachers," or "experts," for enough time to feel empowered with new knowledge and leadership abilities. Students use technology they have learned in previous years as a tool for communication of information and ideas. (Note: In North Carolina, students learn a variety of multimedia technology tools.) They are active learners who control a portion of their learning, who have choices in the country they choose and in how they present it. Ongoing formative assessment and feedback are vital to the success of the team on the "end product." In these ways, this unit incorporates differentiation, culturally responsive pedagogy, "brain-friendly" strategies, and defensible assessment and classroom management.

This unit also provides a template for instruction at any level beyond third grade, but, most importantly, for middle and high school units. Imagine the possibilities in which the student can be in charge of his/her own learning vs. listening to a lecture or reading a textbook chapter and answering questions at the end of the chapter and on a test. Students can research and present, for example, (a) different states or regions of the United States (fifth grade); (b) different regions or historical events in the state (in our case, North Carolina, fourth grade and eighth grade); (c) significant patterns/events/time periods/conflicts in World History (ninth grade); (d) patterns of government and economic principles at local, state, and federal levels (tenth grade); and (e) significant patterns/events/time periods/conflicts in US History (eleventh grade). There is literature available at a variety of reading levels to enrich the unit and support differentiation in all of these potential units. At any of these grade levels, students will learn best when they take charge of their learning.

STUDENT LEARNING OUTCOMES

Knowledge

- After going to the different Durham Stations, describe the historical, cultural, social, economic, and geographic aspects of Durham, NC.
- After researching a country, create a comprehensive learning station that represents the historical, cultural, social, economic, and geographic aspects of various countries around the world.
- After visiting comprehensive learning stations developed by other teams, describe the historical, cultural, social, economic, and geographic aspects of various countries around the world.

Skills

- After reviewing a variety of research skills, use these skills in developing a comprehensive learning station on a specific country.

- Use communication skills—oral, written, and visual—to present a learning station.
- Apply technology skills by using these to enhance the learning station presentation.

Dispositions/Affective

- Identify similarities and differences in other ways of living and believing, as compared to our own life style, environment, and belief systems.
- Describe, illustrate, and/or demonstrate the complex dynamics that define/characterize a group (history, culture, ethnicity, language, region), while maintaining a realization of individuality within groups.

RESEARCH FOUNDATIONS OF THIS UNIT

Renzulli's Enrichment Triad Model (1977) provides the foundation for this unit by beginning with general exploratory activities; providing training in creativity, critical thinking and problem solving; and finally, becoming a researcher/investigator (Baum 1988). While not a "real" problem identified as a personal area of interest and investigation by the students, as suggested in Renzulli's model, greater understanding of others is a real challenge in our world an provides a valid curricular focus for this unit. Future success depends on students' ability to understand and empathize with others.

The unit, using Renzulli's definition of "giftedness," addresses the intellectual (above-average ability), artistic (creativity), and social domains (task commitment) of his model (Gagne, 1985). *Moreover*, these domains are essential to planning a differentiated curriculum that addresses the strengths and needs of *all* learners.

Table 4.1 is an advance organizer of the activities in this unit, arranged according to Nunley's (2004) Layered Curriculum. This is followed by a feature matrix for the Durham Stations, and then by a model of how the Durham Stations leads to Country Stations.

TABLE 4.1   Advance Organizer of Activities Arranged According to Nunley's (2004) Layered Curriculum

Components	Layer C: Know & Comprehend	Layer B: Apply & Analyze	Layer A: Evaluate & Create
Durham Stations	1. Write notes about each station in the Travel Guide *and/or* 2. Write notes on the feature matrix for the stations	Choice assignment: 1. Write an essay about one of the stations. 2. Compare two stations.	Choice assignment: 1. Create a Foldable®, PowerPoint, brochure, etc. to present what you have learned on this "fieldtrip." 2. Draw a timeline using the stations and write in key information/events about each. (This could be a Foldable® timeline.) 3. Write a story based on one of the sites/time periods.
Research & Skills		1. Identify key questions as a guide to research. 2. Collect and record resources in correct bibliographical form. 3. Plan roles of team members. 4. Organize information using graphic organizers (including Foldables®) 5. Display key information using text. 6. Display information using visuals. 7. Plan for music, movement/dance, food, etc.	
Countries	1. Write notes about each country in the Passport *and/or* 2. Write notes on the feature matrix of countries		1. Create a comprehensive learning station about your country 2. Evaluate the effectiveness of the information and presentation of the other country stations you visited 3. Evaluate the effectiveness of your own station and of the team and each team member

DURHAM STATIONS MATRIX AND WORKSHEET

What does the place below and the people associated with the place tell you about the history, social life, economy, and culture of the community?

	Historical	Social	Economic	Cultural
Hayti (including Lincoln Health Center, Stanford Warren Library)				
North Carolina Central University				
NC Mutual and "Black Wall Street"				
Duke University, the Dukes, and Duke Homestead				
Today's Durham (e.g., Research Triangle Park, Durham Bulls baseball Stadium, Southpoint Mall, Downtown,)				
Bennett Place				
Duke Homestead				
Stagville and Horton Grove				

OVERVIEW OF RELATIONSHIP BETWEEN
DURHAM STATIONS AND COUNTRY STATIONS

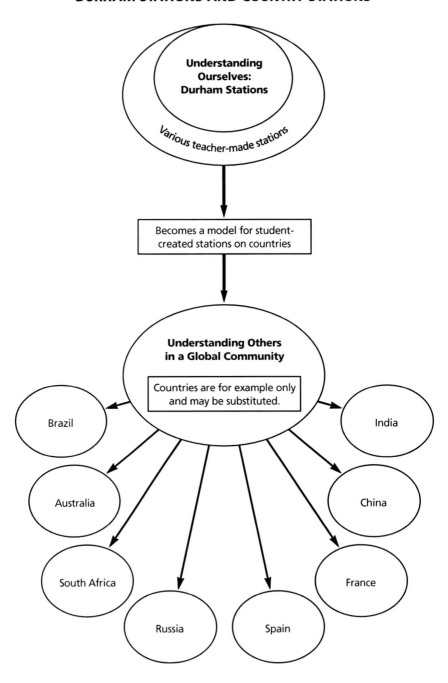

GENERAL OVERVIEW OF THE UNIT

This unit is described as a two-week, full-day program which could be implemented in the summer or on a special schedule at the beginning or end-of-year program. If the unit was implemented as a class period or in the Social Studies and/or Language arts block, the timing would have to be adjusted for shorter daily time periods.

First, I will describe the program in a general overview; then, I will detail the day-by-day activities. For the first three days, after some initial class— and team—building activities, the students learn about the history and culture of Durham, a place where they live but may not know very much about. Oftentimes, people take their own culture and community for granted and do not realize its rich stories and roots. A film of the community's history, if one is available, may begin the actual content component. The teacher will research and prepare learning stations with visual displays and presentations about significant historical sites in Durham, addressing the history, culture, economy and social life of the people and place. Each Durham (learning) station should include several of the following—written information, pictures, artifacts, video clips, digital storytelling, game, song, dance, food. The information and visuals may be shared, for example, on a tri-fold display and/or PowerPoint. A digital camcorder might be used to capture an interview with a knowledgeable person at the historical site which can be produced as a podcast (digital storytelling). (Note: Teachers may want to work with grade-level teams to plan different stations (e.g., Stagville Plantation and Horton Grove, Bennett Place) so that students actually travel from classroom to classroom and each teacher/team focuses on one station.)

The teacher will have a "Durham Station" Event, significant in that Durham was once called Durham Station. Students explore these sites/stations as a mock field trip, moving from station to station and gathering information in a Travel Guide booklet or on a feature matrix (see samples at the end of the chapter). They will use this information to create a timeline, Foldable®, brochure, PowerPoint, catalog, story, digital story, essay, or other work product to demonstrate what they have learned from their field trip. This experience will also provide a model for the team studies of different countries that come next.

For the next four days, students engage in structured activities to build skills as well as to have less structured time for researching different countries and cultures around the world. Each team will have a different country. Structured activities include, for example, explaining project expectations and planning, focusing on research skills, and building skills in incorporating technology tools. Each team begins by making a K, W, L chart as a way of focusing what they want to learn and how they may divide up the work to answer all their questions. Teachers present skills, like using research strategies, evaluating resources, looking for important information, using one's own words, and presentation techniques (visual, oral, and written). Presentation techniques may include learning a variety of Foldables®, using some new technology tools, dressing the part, or any other technique that enhances the presentation.

The eighth day will involve putting the final presentation and displays together. The last two days will be the multicultural culminating event. Parents, school district representatives, and university guests should be invited to take this "trip around the world," seeing the fruits of the students' labor.

The following is the daily agenda for this unit, including activities and rubrics:

Day 1—Opening, Stage Setting, and Team Building

- Welcome, Introductions, Icebreakers, explanation of program, students indicate top three choices of countries—whole group
  - Sample Icebreaker—Students stand in a circle, facing in. Each student gives an adjective and his/her name (e.g., Shy Sharon, Jazzy Jasmine, Lovable Laura). Each person must say his or her name with an adjective and, then, repeat all the previous names with adjectives (e.g., Jazzy Jasmine must say her name and adjective and "Shy Sharon;" Lovable Laura must say her name and adjective, "Jazzy Jasmine, Shy Sharon").
- Divide into teams by countries.
- Team—and class—building activities
  - Class-building requires getting up, moving around, and working with everyone.
    1. Using Favorites Cards, students will walk around asking different students about, for example, their favorite color, flavor of ice cream, song.
    2. Using a *Find Someone Who . . .* worksheet, students walk around and look for someone who . . . has an older sister, knows how to knit. Several items are listed on the worksheet and students sign beside an item that applies to them (each student can only sign beside one item on someone else's worksheet).
  - Team building is fun, easy, and does not include content.
    1. Using *All About Me* Cards, students in teams of four take turns asking and answering questions to share information about themselves to get to know each other better.

- Film—*Negro Durham Marches On* (Durham Public Library, Main Branch, Audio-Visual Collection) or another video/DVD about the community
- Divide back into teams; small group discussions on film.
  - What time period is illustrated in this film? How do you know?
  - Describe some of the images from the film.
  - Have you been to any of the places in the film? How have these places changed?
  - From whose perspective is this film presented? Why do you think this was done?
  - What is missing? Having viewed the film and given your current experiences in Durham, what can you surmise about the other cultural groups in the community during the time the film was made?
  - What did you learn about Durham that you did not know before?
  - How did you feel about the film? Why?

Days 2–3 Durham Stations (mock field trip)

- Students visit Durham Stations developed by teacher/teams. A full station set-up within a classroom or a station per classroom, created by a teacher or teams of teachers, provides opportunities for substantive interaction on the part of students. However, due to space, stations may be presented as comprehensive poster displays, along with mini-lesson(s)/presentations, and/or other experiences and guest speakers.
- Students complete a Travel Guide (catalog) OR feature matrix (below) as they visit different stations. The Travel Guide allows the student to create a "catalog" of information, but the feature matrix (which can be made from a Foldable®) allows the student to see the information across stations for each category. Students visit four stations each of the two days allocated for this activity.

Durham Stations Travel Guide Rubric

Ratings: 3 = effective; 2 = acceptable; 1 = not acceptable; 0 = not completed

This rubric is for the evaluation of information students write in travel guides or on the feature matrix, not for the evaluation of actual stations.

	Historical	Social	Economic	Cultural
Hayti (including Lincoln Health Center, Stanford Warren Library)				
North Carolina Central University				
NC Mutual Building and "Black Wall Street"				
Duke University, the Dukes, and Duke Homestead				
Today's Durham (Research Triangle Park, Durham Bulls Baseball Stadium, Southpoint Mall, Downtown)				
Bennett Place				
Duke Homestead				
Stagville and Horton Grove				

After visiting all stations, students write an essay about one station or a comparison/contrast of two stations.

Compare/Contrast Essay Rubric

	Exemplary	Effective	Acceptable	Unacceptable
Content	Main thesis is clear and insightful with three elements of similarity and three elements of difference	Main thesis is clear with three elements of similarity and two elements of difference	Main thesis is somewhat clear with two elements of similarity and two elements of difference	Main thesis is not clear and/or includes only one element of similarity and/or one element of difference
Coherence and organization	Ideas are well connected, logical, and use clear transitions	Ideas are connected, logical, and use appropriate transitions	Ideas are loosely connected, and may not consistently use clear transitions	Ideas are choppy, illogical, disjointed, and/or lacking transitions
Correctness	No major or minor errors in punctuation, spelling, grammar	No major and only minimal minor errors in punctuation, spelling, grammar	No major and only a few minor errors in punctuation, spelling, grammar	Major and/or significant minor errors in punctuation, spelling, grammar
Creativity	Meets assignment requirements and displays a great deal of creativity	Meets assignment requirements and displays some level of creativity	Meets assignment requirements, but displays little or no creativity	Barely meets assignment requirements, and displays little creativity

Scoring: Add up points earned _____ divide by 4 = _____ Final score

Days 4–7 Research, Skill Building, and Literature Enrichment

- With respect to Durham Stations, students will choose one of the following assignments:
  - Write a story based on one of the sites/time periods.
  - Create a Foldable®, PowerPoint, brochure, catalog, or other visual display to present what you have learned on this "fieldtrip."
  - Draw a timeline using the stations and write in key information/events about each. (This could be a Foldable® timeline.)

Rubrics for the story, essay, and timeline are provided below.

Story Rubric

	Exemplary	Effective	Acceptable	Unacceptable
Text	Story is exceptionally coherent, clear and creatively executed with attention to detail. Dialogue is effectively and *creatively* used to support the story.	Story is coherent and clear; writer has obviously taken time to develop images. Dialogue is effectively used to support the story.	Story is coherent and generally developed, using some dialogue to support the story.	Story is either not connected or is only loosely connected; not clear or well-developed; and therefore, only minimally coherent.
Structure*	Includes and fully develops all parts of a story *and* has multiple attempts and outcomes or multiple goals, with attempts and outcomes.	Includes and fully develops all parts of a story	Includes most parts of a story, but may not be fully developed	Either includes and develops some parts *or* includes most parts but they are loosely connected and not well developed.
Overall	Structure and text are effectively and creatively working together to provide a rich story.	Structure and text effectively work together to provide a good story.	Structure and text are coherent and somewhat developed to provide a modest story.	Structure and text are not well developed and only loosely connected; therefore, this is a weak story.

Scoring: Add up points earned _____ divide by 3 = _____ Final score

* Based on Mandler and Johnson's (1977) Story Grammar, the parts of the story include (a) setting; (b) beginning or initiating event; (c) reaction (to the beginning/initiating event); (d) goal(s); (e) attempt(s); (f) outcome(s); and (g) resolution/ending.

Essay Rubric

	Exemplary	Effective	Acceptable	Unacceptable
Content	Main thesis is clear and insightful; all evidence supports thesis	Main thesis is clear and evidence typically supports thesis	Main thesis is somewhat clear and evidence generally supports thesis	Main thesis is not clear and evidence is sketchy
Coherence and Organization	Ideas are well connected, logical, and use clear transitions	Ideas are connected, logical, and use appropriate transitions	Ideas are loosely connected, and may not consistently use clear transitions	Ideas are choppy, illogical, disjointed, and/or lacking transitions
Accuracy	No major or minor errors in punctuation, spelling, grammar	No major and only minimal minor errors in punctuation, spelling, grammar	No major and only a few minor errors in punctuation, spelling, grammar	Major and/or significant minor errors in punctuation, spelling, grammar
Creativity	Meets assignment requirements and displays a great deal of creativity	Meets assignment requirements and displays some level of creativity	Meets assignment requirements, but displays little or no creativity	Barely meets assignment requirements, and displays little creativity

Scoring: Add up points earned _____ divide by 4 = _____ Final score

Timeline Rubric

	Exemplary	Effective	Acceptable	Unacceptable
Content	All events are included and described clearly, chronologically, and insightfully	Most events are included and described clearly and chronologically	Most events are included and are described somewhat clearly and chronologically	A limited number of events are included and/or the events included are not clear and/or chronological
Accuracy	No major or minor errors in punctuation, spelling, grammar	No major and only minimal minor errors in punctuation, spelling, grammar	No major and only a few minor errors in punctuation, spelling, grammar	Major and/or significant minor errors in punctuation, spelling, grammar
Creativity	Meets assignment requirements and displays a great deal of creativity	Meets assignment requirements and displays some level of creativity	Meets assignment requirements, but displays little or no creativity	Barely meets assignment requirements, and displays little creativity

Scoring: Add up points earned _____ divide by 4 = _____ Final score

Day 4–7 Research, Skill Building, and Literature Enrichment for Country Stations (continued)

- With respect to the Country Project, explain to students that they will work on a team to create a comprehensive learning station for their country (one of their three choices of countries to study). Provide examples of the various presentation modes and technologies used in Durham stations as options for students in presenting their countries. Discuss the *Assessment Rubric for Country Project,* shown below.

Assessment Rubric for Country Project

	Exemplary	Effective	Acceptable	Unacceptable
Art	Well-planned, visually/musically creative, highly original, thought-provoking, and well-integrated with written component	Well-planned, visually or musically creative, well-connected to written component	Planned, supports and is connected to written component	Not well-planned and/or not well-connected to written component, but included
Writing	Clear, concise, convincing, and creative with no major and virtually no grammatical/mechanical errors	Clear, concise, and convincing with no major and limited grammatical/mechanical errors	Clear and concise with minimal major or minor errors	Not clear or concise and/or has a number of major/minor errors that interfere with meaning
Technology	Uses technology effectively and creatively to enhance presentation	Uses technology effectively	Uses technology	Uses technology ineffectively or does not use it at all
Research	Uses at least 6 resources and lists them in correct bibliographical form	Uses 4–5 resources and lists in correct bibliographical form	Uses 3 resources and lists in almost correct bibliographical form	Uses 2 or fewer resources and/or may not use an acceptable bibliographical form
Presentation	Well-prepared and delivered, capturing the audience	Well-prepared and delivered	Prepared and delivered	Not well-prepared and/or delivered
Overall	Comprehensive, thoroughly researched, creatively designed, appropriately integrated technology, and well presented	Fairly comprehensive, supported by research, technology incorporated, and well presented	Somewhat comprehensive and based on research, technology used, and presented	Not comprehensive, research-based, inappropriate/no use of technology, and/or not presented well

Scoring: Add up points earned _____ divide by 6 = _____ Final score

Day 4—Country Stations

- K–W–L (*Know–Want to Know–Learned* graphic organizer): Within teams, students will complete a K–W–L chart, identifying/recording collective knowledge of the team about their country and forming questions about what they want to know.
- Skill Building (e.g., research skills, evaluating resources, using one's own words, technology applications, Foldable®). Skill building lessons should be kept to thirty-minute sessions. During the first skill building session, discuss and provide models/examples for:
  - Finding resources—library, Internet;
  - Evaluating the credibility of resources;
  - Listing resources in a bibliography;
  - Creating information cards (with bibliographical references)— model how to summarize facts and ideas, putting them into one's own words.
- Research time—provide students with at least two hours—one hour on the first day to go to the library and use the Internet and another hour to begin reading materials. The teacher should circulate and keep anecdotal notes of each team's progress and intervene to provide feedback and direction, as needed.
- Skill Building—provide students with opportunities to learn Foldable® or other creative display strategies. This may require an hour or more, but should be interactive.
- Introduce literature options for various countries. A list is provided at the end of this chapter. Teams should then select books. The team can choose to read the same book; or, two team members can read one book while two read another; or, each person on the team can choose his/her own book (if there are enough choices for the team's country). Students should set reading goals for each day, begin reading if time permits, and finish readings for homework.

Day 5

- In teams, students should indicate which questions have been answered on the K–W–L chart as a review of what they have learned so far and to make a plan for what information they may still need.
- Research time—Teams review their unanswered questions and begin researching those questions. New questions should be posted on the K–W–L chart and additional information *learned* while researching should be recorded on note cards.
- Skill building: (technology tools): Introduce desktop publishing options with samples. The teacher should indicate a schedule of

when these will be offered on Day 5 and 6, during an extended research time. (This would be a great way to involve the technology and media specialists at the school.) Students should attend at least two skill-building sessions on technologies they might want to incorporate into their country's station. Teams may decide to send a representative to different sessions, but each student must attend two. These would include creating (a) a brochure; (b) a Power-Point; (c) a digital storybook; (d) a catalog; or (e) a podcast. If the teacher is responsible for modeling the various technology tools, the schedule should include thirty minutes per tool with thirty minutes between technology tool sessions, so that the teacher can circulate and assist students who are researching (e.g., creating brochures; circulating, assisting, and providing feedback; using PowerPoint; circulating, assisting, and providing feedback; creating a digital storybook...).

- Literature time: Students write a short summary of the selection they have read so far and list any words they were unsure of. They should set new reading goals and continue reading.

Day 6

- Students write letters to invite parents, administrators, school district and other guests inviting them to the Days 9–10 culminating event.
- Research time: Teams review their unanswered questions on K-W-L chart and begin researching those questions. New questions should be posted on the chart and additional information *learned* while researching should be recorded on note cards. Since the information they are learning will be shared in a variety of ways (e.g., models, displays, games), the teams need to begin to plan how the country station will look and list, gather, or create materials to put together in the station on Days 7 and 8.
- Skill building: Interviewing primary resources and experts: The teacher should facilitate a discussion of interview protocol, including (a) planning what questions to ask a primary resource/expert in advance; (b) making contact and scheduling an appointment;

(c) being prepared with necessary equipment and getting permission for audio- or video-taping; and (d) ending an interview and thanking the interviewee. Students should take some time to draft a few questions in their teams, share their ideas with the class, and receive feedback on the appropriateness and effectiveness of their questions in gaining information for their country study.
- Literature: Students write a short summary of the selection they have read so far and list any words they were unsure of. They should set new reading goals and continue reading.

Day 7

- Teams begin creating their presentation displays for their country stations.
- Teams rehearse dances, "speeches," songs, game demonstrations that they have planned for their country station presentation.
- Literature: Students write a short summary of the selection they have read so far and list any words they were unsure of. They should set new reading goals and continue reading.

Day 8—Final Preparations—Putting It All Together

- Teams finish displays and double check everything to ensure that all equipment is available and working, technology projects are complete, and materials for the audience are available.
- Teams rehearse dances, "speeches," songs, games, and demonstrations.
- Literature: Students create a book review which summarizes the story (without giving away the ending) and rates the book on quality and popularity/appeal (see VOYA Review model, p. 90). This should be a visual that becomes a part of the station. If more than one book is read by the team, each book should have a book review.

SAMPLE VOYA REVIEW

Friction. E.R. Frank, New York: Simon Pulse (an imprint of Simon and Schuster). 2003. ISBN: 0-689-85385-8.

Genre: Realistic Fiction
Age Span: 11–18

Quality   5Q: Hard to imagine it being better written.
Popularity 5P: Every young adult was dying to read it yesterday.

Summary: Sometimes, we're challenged to determine where the truth begins and ends. Some lies are easier to recognize than others. When Stacy comes to Forest Alternative School, her "lies" stir up lots of trouble for Alex, her peers, and teacher. Alex tries to ignore Stacy's lies; then, Alex tries to tell Stacy to quit spreading lies. In the end, Alex realizes that Stacy lies and creates friction to keep her own painful secret.

Critical Evaluation/Review: *Friction* rubs raw the senses of emerging teenagers as they rappel into situations that soon take on a life of their own. In this highly believable story about the friction that is caused by the lies one girl tells, all the characters, especially the main character, learn truths hard for anyone, at any age, to imagine. E.R. Frank masterfully presents a common situation, a teenager's rumors, and how those begin to create a friction that ends up "burning" everyone in one way or another, but out of which comes true revelations about friendship, people, and life. As Simon, the teacher, points out— "Behind every lie there is a grain of truth."

Personal Notes: Wow! This was powerful! And so well written.

Days 9–10 A Multicultural Field Trip (Culminating Event)

- Four stations should be visited each day. Students complete a Passport catalog or feature matrix (similar to the one on page 82, but with countries instead of Durham Stations), writing information they learn as they visit each of the country stations.

Passports Rubric

Ratings: 3 = effective; 2 = acceptable; 1 = not acceptable; 0 = not completed

This rubric is for the evaluation of information students write in passports or on the feature matrix, not for the evaluation of actual stations.

	Historical	Social	Economic	Cultural
Australia				
Brazil				
China				
France				
India				
Russia				
Spain				
South Africa				

- Students and visitors will have time to visit the stations and complete their passports (which should be stamped with a team-selected design relevant to the country, like a real passport, as they enter each country). Sample stamps included here are for China and for Spain. Stamps or stickers may be purchased from any teacher supply store.

China   **Spain**

- Students will evaluate each station using the same rubric as the teacher (see **Assessment Rubric for Country Project,** from Day 4 introduction of country learning stations project; process described below), which will give feedback to the various teams. Additionally, they will evaluate their own team's effectiveness in preparing and presenting a country, using the same rubric (see description below).

Rubric for Evaluation of Each Station

- Students will use the *Assessment Rubric for Country Project* for each station, writing the country on the paper and checking the appropriate descriptor for each criterion. On the back of the paper, each student will use a "3–2–1" strategy; students will write three things they liked best, two suggestions for improvement, and one way they grew from this station. Students then paperclip their four evaluations (per day) and attach a sticky note with their name, so the teacher can account for their input. The teacher will complete a rubric and review and compile student evaluation rubrics to give to each team.

Three things that went well	Two ways to improve the project	One way that I grew personally
1.	1.	1.
2.	2.	
3.		

Team Member	Overall Rating	Reason

Rubric for Evaluation of Own Project

Students will use the *Assessment Rubric for Overall Project* for their own station, writing the country and "self-evaluation" on the paper and checking the appropriate descriptor for each criterion.

On the back of the paper, each student will use the "3–2–1" strategy, writing at least three things they thought went really well on the project, two ways they could have improved the project, and one way they each changed personally from this experience.

They should rate the contributions of each team member and indicate why they rated each team member as they did. For this purpose, the back of the assessment rubric will include two small tables (see p. 92); each would be expanded to provide room for responding.

SUMMARY

In Chapter 4: *Community and Culture—Understanding Ourselves and Others in the Global Community,* students learned about the historical, political, economic and social community in which they live. This experience provided them with models for researching and developing comprehensive learning stations, so that they, in teams, could develop a comprehensive learning station about a country to teach to other teams, who also did the same. Students learned and practiced research, technology, and presentation skills to enhance their ability to learn about and teach others about their country. Reading and researching in this unit came from a variety of sources—for example, brochures, pamphlets, books, the Internet, videos, and interviews. There were many opportunities for informal and formal writing. Equally as important as the content knowledge gained and the research, technology, and literacy skills developed was their chance to develop a greater awareness about themselves and others around the world beyond mere "food, fun, and festivals."

BOOKS

A primary resource for the list of books to be used in this unit is Anita Silvey's (2006) *500 Great Books for Teens.* Silvey includes books from a variety of geographical locations, which would also support a different selection of countries. Several of the books have been referenced and read by the authors of *The Perfect Norm.*

Africa

Feelings, Tom. (1995) *The Middle Passage: White Ships, Black Cargo.* Dial. (80 pages, an adult picture book)
Stratton, Allan. (2004) *Chanda's Secret.* Annick Press. (176 pages)

Botswana
Smith, Alexander McCall. (2002) *The No. 1 Ladies Detective Agency.* Anchor. (235 pages)

Somalia
Bowden, Mark. (1999) *Black Hawk Down: A Story of Modern War.* Atlantic. (486 pages)

South Africa
Coman, Carolyn. (2000) *Many Stones.* Front Street. (158 pages)
Fugard, Athol. (1982) *"Master Harold" . . . and the boys.* Knopf. (60 pages, a play).
Rochman, Hazel. (1988) *Somehow Tenderness Survives: Stories of Southern Africa.* Harper. (147 pages)

Asia

China
Hwang, David Henry. (1998). *Golden Child.* New York: Theater Communications Group, Inc. (62 pages, a play)
Ji-Li, Jiang. (1997). *The Red Scarf Girl: A Memoir of the Cultural Revolution.* Harper Collins Publisher. (304 pages)
Sijie, Dai. (2001) *Balzac and the Little Chinese Seamstress.* Knopf. (208 pages)

Japan
Mori, Kyoko. (1993) *Shizuko's Daughter.* Holt. (238 pages)
Uchida, Yoshiko. (2005). *Journey to Topaz.* Heydey Books. (160 pages)

Korea
Na, An (2001). *A Step From Heaven.* Front Street Press. (156 pages)
Park, Linda Sue. (2002) *When My Name Was Keoko.* Clarion. (201 pages)
Watkins, Yoko Kawashima. (1986) *So Far From the Bamboo Grove.* Lothrop. (184 pages)

Vietnam
Myers, Walter Dean. (1988) *Fallen Angels.* Scholastic. (309 pages)
O'Brien, Tim. (1990) *The Things They Carried.* Houghton Mifflin. (272 pages)

Australia

Hartnett, Sonya. (1995) *Sleeping Dogs.* Viking. (133 pages)
Marsden, John. (1994) *Letters from the Inside.* Houghton Mifflin. (160 pages)
Marsden, John. (1995) *Tomorrow, When the War Began.* Houghton Mifflin. (286 pages)
Moriarty, Jaclyn. (2004) *The Year of Secret Assignments.* Scholastic/Levine. (344 pages)
Zusak, Markus. (2005) *I Am The Messenger.* Knopf. (359 pages)

France

Brown, Dan. (2003) *The Da Vinci Code.* Doubleday. (454 pages)
Elliott, L.M. (2001) *Under the War-Torn Sky.* Hyperion. (284 pages)
Moser, Richard.(2001) *Zazoo.* Clarion. (266 pages)
Sedaris, David. (2000) *Me Talk Pretty One Day.* Little, Brown. (272 pages)
Spillebeen, Geert. (2005) *Kipling's Choice.* Houghton Mifflin. (160 pages)

India

Lahiri, Jhumpa. (1999) *Interpreter of Maladies.* Houghton Mifflin. (198 pages)
Martel, Yann.(2001) *Life of Pi.* Harcourt. (401 pages)
Whelan, Gloria. (2000) *Homeless Bird.* HarperCollins. (192 pages)

Russia

Holub, Josef. (2005) *An Innocent Soldier.* Scholastic/Levine. (232 pages)
Wulffson, Don. (2001) *Soldier X.* Viking. (227 pages)

Spain

Coehlo, Paulo. (1993) *The Alchemist.* Harper. (173 pages)
Zafón, Carlos Ruíz. (2001; translation by Lucia Graves, 2004) *The Shadow of The Wind.* Penguin. (487 pages)

South America
(Brazil—no books specifically listed for Brazil)

Márquez, Gabriel García. (1970) *One Hundred Years of Solitude.* Harper. (383 pages)

REFERENCES

Baum, S. (1988). An enrichment program for gifted learning disabled students. *Gifted Education Quarterly, 32*(1), 226–230.

Friedman, T. L. (2005). *The world is flat: A brief history of the twenty-first century.* New York: Farrar, Straus & Giroux.

Gagné, F. (1985). Giftedness and talent: Reexamining a reexamination of the definitions. *Gifted Education Quarterly, 29*(3), 103–112.

Mandler, J. M., & Johnson, N. S. (1977). Remembrance of things parsed: Story structure and recall. *Cognitive Psychology, 9,* 111–151.

Nunley, K. F. (2004). *Layered curriculum*™ (2nd ed.). Amherst, NH: Brains.org.

Renzulli, J. S. (1977). *The enrichment triad model: A guide for developing defensible program for the gifted and talented.* Mansfield Center, CT: Creative Learning Press.

Silvey, A. (2006). *500 great books for teens.* Boston: Houghton Mifflin Co.

CHAPTER 5

A JOURNEY FROM INNOCENCE TO EXPERIENCE

A Course in Young Adult Literature for Future Teachers

INTRODUCTION

Depth and breadth of knowledge about young adult books (also referred to as adolescent literature) and characteristics of the various genres are essential knowledge for beginning English/language arts teachers. Just as each

The Perfect Norm, pages 97–115
Copyright © 2009 by Information Age Publishing
All rights of reproduction in any form reserved.

teacher will have his or her own preferences in genre, students will have their own preferences. For teachers and students alike, preferences are often a result of what we know; therefore, we need to make a concerted effort to expose ourselves to a wide variety of genres in order to expand our preferences. Since teachers (and media specialists) often serve as a resource for students about books, teachers must maintain an up-to-date awareness of contemporary, as well as classic, young adult literature.

I had the opportunity to begin teaching a Young Adult Literature course a few years ago. Luckily, I was able to register for this course under the tutelage of the professor from whom I would take over the course. This was a scary proposition since the professor was highly regarded by students, almost a force of nature. Despite my anxious anticipation, I was excited to learn from the "best." It was she who led me on this journey of immersing myself in young adult literature. She continues to encourage me by sending me young adult books from time-to-time. Many of the activities in the syllabus presented here have been adapted from her syllabus. However, I have re-shaped the syllabus into a layered curriculum, adding some choices here and there, to make it my own. Interestingly, the *Choices* unit in this book was originally developed as an assignment when I took the Young Adult Literature course. Now, her assignment to *develop a unit* has become "Layer B" of my syllabus. Thus, one teacher has passed on her wisdom to another and I, in turn, pass it on to you.

This course is a work in progress. Admittedly, it has proven to be quite a lot of work for candidates nearing the end of their teacher preparation program, when they also take several other high-level English courses. However, the work is fun, despite the assignment load, *if* students keep up.

Within this unit, I engage students in learning teams for various types of activities, giving them choices in their work and in the presentation of that work. For example, in literature circles, teams read different short stories. All teams complete four tasks: (a) summarize the story; (b) identify unknown vocabulary, (c) write key questions (and answers) that others should be able to answer after reading the story; and (d) draw a picture to represent the story or a part of the story. In some cases, teams complete graphic organizers about the characters or the story's plot.

For the realistic fiction assignment, students had to read a book as a team and put together some sort of presentation to share their book with other teams. The purpose was three-fold. First, teams read one book in-depth. Second, teams discussed, analyzed, and determined how to familiarize others with that book. The presentations were more than a book talk to inspire others to read the book, but not as involved as a full analysis. Third, as a result of the presentations, teams learned from their peers about other books in the realistic fiction genre. I taught them how to make Foldables® as one option for creating a visual presentation, but they could create a

PowerPoint or any other visual display to accompany their presentations. In pairs, students chose a category of non-fiction (e.g., information books, how-to books, self-help books), explored various titles in their selected non-fiction category, and created a visual to present four of those titles using the following components for each book: (a) summary/ description of book; (b) author information and credibility (Is there evidence that the author has the knowledge and experience to write about the topic?); (c) statement about young adult appeal of the book; and (d) response to key questions based on the specific category (included on Layered Curriculum Chart in syllabus).

As can be seen in the examples I have given above, students were often engaged in "brain-friendly" strategies. They used *cooperative learning; brainstormed and discussed* ideas related to young adult literature (topics, genre, and specific books); created *visuals;* included *drawing and artwork;* used *technology* to create *visuals, write,* and *reflect;* and used *graphic organizers* (both two- and three-dimensional [Foldables®]). Additionally, students engaged in *storytelling* and reciprocal *teaching* via team work and shared the books they read for these assignments. Students *visualized* as they listened to the stories others shared about the books they were reading. Students read and shared books in the *humor* category. With respect to *humor* and to *music, rhythm, rhyme and rap,* students created a poetry collection that included silly and humorous poems; lyrics, which could include rap; and rhyming or non-rhyming poetry. They went on *field trips* to the local public, or school, library and bookstores to determine what was available and to check out/ buy books for assignments. All in all, of the twenty "brain-friendly" strategies, at least twelve were used in this unit.

STUDENT LEARNING OUTCOMES FOR THE UNIT

The student learning outcomes listed below are in the course syllabus. In teacher education, students are referred to as "candidates" to distinguish them from the pre-kindergarten through twelfth-grade public school students they will serve.

1. After reading the course text and young adult literature in various genres, the candidate will apply the characteristics of each genre and evaluate the literature in writing (e.g., paper, graphic organizer, etc.), as a discussion forum, or as a presentation.
2. Given information about the history of young adult literature, the candidate will develop a timeline or chronology of significant developments.

3. Using experiences with students in schools and the community, reviewing young adult sections of book stores and libraries, and reading young adult literature, candidates will discuss cultural trends which affect young adult reading interests.
4. After surveying bookstores and libraries, as well as reading text chapters and a variety of books, the candidate will identify important authors of young adult literature.
5. As each genre is explored, candidates will identify titles of accepted genres in the body of young adult literature and create a book file with a summary and critical review of each book read based on the characteristics of each genre.
6. After selecting a theme relevant to young adults, the candidate will create an integrated unit demonstrating uses of young adult literature in English, reading, and social studies classrooms.
7. After reading a variety of current books and reviewing the chapter on censorship, the candidate will describe taboos and censorship issues related to young adult literature.
8. At the end of the course, candidate will articulate a personal philosophy about the value of young adult literature.

OVERVIEW OF THE UNIT

The Unit is a syllabus, and, thus, is written like a typical university syllabus. Minimally, it includes the course number and title; meeting day and time; instructor and contact information; course description; required text(s); assignments and evaluation; and bibliography/suggested readings. The syllabus below includes some components that are unique to teacher education and/or me. Teacher education syllabi typically include a conceptual framework—ours is *Preparing Educators for Diverse Cultural Contexts* – which is regularly reviewed, updated, and expanded based on current literature in the field. As a former public school teacher, I have always included "expectations" about behavior, like *treat other class members respectfully at all times and particularly during presentations and discussions*. In this day and time, "expectations" must also include statements about turning off cell phones.

The course description clearly indicates *culturally responsive pedagogy* in three ways. First, the *wide range of genres* meets the variety of preferences in the classroom. Second, the inclusion of *multi-cultural literature* addresses cultural differences and perspectives. Third, the use of a *variety of pedagogy and assessment strategies* makes learning accessible regardless of learning differences.

As previously indicated, the assignments have been re-shaped into a layered curriculum. In Layer C, students must read the textbook and examples of the various genres, demonstrating comprehension in many different ways. In Layer B, students must apply what they have learned about books to develop a teaching unit. In Layer A, students create a rationale for teaching a book and/or including a particular book in a reading list and evaluate that book using the VOYA style of review. In a VOYA Review, the writer includes a rating (1–5, with 5 being the highest) for quality and one for popularity/appeal to young adults, and a justification for each rating.

More and more middle and high schools expect their teachers to develop course syllabi to define the course-of-study for the students. Additionally, with a greater focus on a seamless grade six through fourteen, some students are moving through the curriculum at a faster pace and are taking two years of college courses prior to graduating from high school. This provides a model for how a teacher can differentiate instruction, incorporate principles of cognitive psychology and neuroscience research, and use culturally responsive pedagogy. Ultimately, such practices result in defensible assessment and ethical classroom management.

THE UNIT/SYLLABUS

Preparing Educators for Diverse Cultural Contexts

EDU 4950: Special Topics in Education
Young Adult Literature
Mondays 4:00–6:30 p.m.
Spring 2008

Instructor's Name   919-530-xxxx
School of Education xxxx   e-mail: xxxxxxx@nccu.edu

Course Description

This course provides a historical perspective on and characteristics of various genres within young adult literature. Candidates read, analyze, synthesize, and evaluate young adult literature in each genre. Literature has been selected to represent various cultures and belief systems to expose candidates to literature representative of the students they may serve in their classrooms, to encourage candidates to use multi-cultural literature in their classrooms, and to have candidates explore their own perceptions with respect to other cultures and beliefs. Candidates will use a variety of strategies to demonstrate knowledge, skills and dispositions, including, but not limited to, papers, book talks, timelines and other graphic organizers, desktop publishing (catalogues, brochures), Powerpoint, discussion forums, and presentations.

Course Texts (required)

Donelson, Kenneth L. and Nilsen, Alleen Pace. *Literature for Today's Young Adults.* 7th ed. Pearson, Allyn and Bacon, 2005.

Student Learning Outcomes

1. After reading the course text and young adult literature in various genres, the candidate will apply the characteristics of each genre and evaluate the literature in writing (e.g., paper, graphic organizer), as a discussion forum, or as a presentation.
2. Given information about the history of young adult literature, the candidate will develop a timeline or chronology of significant developments.
3. Using experiences with students in schools and the community, reviewing young adult sections of book stores and libraries, and reading young adult literature, candidates will discuss cultural trends which affect young adult reading interests.
4. After surveying bookstores and libraries, as well as reading text chapters and a variety of books, the candidate will identify important authors of young adult literature.
5. As each genre is explored, candidates will identify titles of accepted genres in the body of young adult literature and create a book file with a summary and critical review of each book read, based on the characteristics of each genre.
6. After selecting a theme relevant to young adults, the candidate will create an integrated unit demonstrating uses of young adult literature in English, reading, and social studies classrooms.
7. After reading a variety of current books and reviewing the chapter on censorship, the candidate will describe taboos and censorship issues related to young adult literature.
8. At the end of the course, candidates will articulate a personal philosophy about the value of young adult literature.

Assessment and Evaluation

While assignments will be submitted via digital dropbox or discussion board, you are expected to create an e-portfolio of these course assignments and the book file. All assignments must be submitted by the due date for full credit.

Course Assignments include reading books and chapters, presentations, PowerPoints, timelines, literature circle packets, and short papers as assigned per topic.

Book File—A write-up is required for each book read in completion of chapter assignments and should include the following:

> Bibliographic information (including ISBN)
>
> Genre
>
> Approximate age span for which the book is appropriate
>
> Summary (2–5 sentences)
>
> Critical Evaluation (apply criteria for genre learned from text readings)
>
> Personal notes (What impact, if any, did the book have on you? Would you use the book in your teaching?)

This file is due on April 30 via digital dropbox. Please complete individual entries as you read each book.

The point value for assignments is as follows. Each assignment must be completed at Layer C to submit work at Layer B, and each Layer B assignment must be completed to submit Layer A assignments. Assignments at each layer are expected to be thoughtfully developed and carefully executed.

- Course assignments
  - Layer C (each assignment 3 points)   60 points
  - Layer B (each assignment 5 points)   10 points
  - Layer A (each assignment 5 points)   10 points
- Book file (1 point per book)   <u>20 points</u>
                                      TOTAL   100 points

Other Important Information

Candidates are expected to
- Be on time for class;
- Attend regularly;
- Make friends with a class member to get notes in the event that an absence is unavoidable;
- Treat other class members respectfully at all times and particularly during presentations and discussions;

- Turn cell phones off (or, if absolutely necessary, put on vibrate and answer only for emergencies);
- Check Blackboard **AT LEAST** once per week, if not more;
- Check the NCCU website or Blackboard for class status during inclement weather;
- Register with Office for Students with Disabilities, if accommodations are needed.

TENTATIVE CALENDAR

This course will be web-enhanced via Blackboard. In-class meetings are *mandatory*. In accordance with University policy, candidates will be dropped from this class if they miss more than two class periods, since this course meets only once per week. You should access Blackboard *weekly* for announcements and assignments. All assignments are due on the day of class, unless otherwise noted. *Late assignments will result in reduced credit. You must keep up!*

Use the *discussion forum* to submit (post) assignments, unless directed to use the *digital dropbox* or to submit in class.

LAYER C

| Chapter 1: Understanding Young Adults and Books

Due January 22 | Required:
1. Describe young adult literature, identifying its distinguishing characteristics. Discuss the ways that understanding psychological concepts along with reading young adult literature can help adults.
2. In observance of Martin Luther King, Jr. Day, select a book about MLK, Jr., another Civil Rights activist, or a book about that time period. Read it for value and interest for young adults. Submit your impressions to the Forum.
Choose one and submit to the Forum:
3. Spend time examining the young adult sections in both a school or public library and a bookstore. Report your findings about the young adult market in the libraries and bookstores to the Forum.
4. Spend time examining the young adult sections in both a school or public library and a bookstore. Make a list of 20 titles of the variety of different genres available.
5. Find 5 different websites that support the use of young adult literature. List the sites and briefly describe what they have to offer. | 1 book

Respond to 2 postings (assignment submissions of classmates) |

Chapter 2: A Brief History of Adolescent Literature
 	
Due January 28
	Required:
	1. Develop a timeline of Young Adult Literature, noting the most significant developments. Submit to the Forum and bring to class on **Jan 28.**
	Choose one and submit to the Forum:
	2. Read one of the Stratemeyer Library Syndicate books and consider the following questions:
	   – What assumptions about young adults and young people are inherent in the book?
	   – What assumptions about life and people made the book popular?
	   – Why do you suppose some teachers and librarians have opposed these books?
	   – As an English teacher, would you allow credit for reading a Stratemeyer book? State your reasons.
	3. Review the list of taboos that faced writers of young adult fiction in the 1940s, 1950s, and 1960s. In addition to the reasons mentioned, why do you feel these taboos were certain to disappear with time? Was their disappearance necessarily good for adolescent novels? Skim through current sources to determine if taboos have actually disappeared. Report your findings and conclusions.
		1 book (if you select Choice 2)
		
		Respond to 2 postings

Chapter 3: YA Literature, Pop Culture, and the Mass Media *February 4*	Required: 1. Select a book in the Honors list in Chapter 1 or a recent (2001–2007) Best Books for Young Adults (BBYA) title. Discuss characteristics sited by Dresang (pages 77–79) that appear in your book selection. Document with examples. Submit to the Forum. Choose one and submit to the Forum: 2. Read one of the books in FOCUS BOX 3.1 (p.80) or BOX 3.2 (p. 86) and discuss the effectiveness of what was done. 3. There are children's books which young adults and adults like. There are also picture books written for young adults. Explore and discuss several (3 or more) books in this category (some suggested books in FOCUS BOX 3.3 on p. 96)	2 + books Respond to 2 postings

	Required:	3 books

Chapter 4:
Contemporary
Realistic Fiction:
from Tragedies to
Romances
 	
February 11–25
	1. Read Chapter 4 as a context for discussion on **Feb 11** of *The Chocolate War* and *The Runner* (you will be assigned one of these books to have read by **Feb 11** as well).
	2. Meet with cooperative groups during class time (on **Feb. 11**) to plan book presentation for assigned book (**on Feb 18**). Groups will be assigned.
	  – *The Warriors*
	  – *A Step From Heaven*
	  – *Holes*
	  – *Looking for Alaska*
	Presentations on **Feb. 18** in class should make others want to read your book. Each team member must have a role in the presentation.
	3. Select any book other than a "class read" of this genre. A) Think of a creative way to present your findings (e.g., use a graphic organizer or a foldable). B) List problems that young adults have and the difficult decisions they must make. How do they compare with those of young adults in any generation? Submit to the Forum by **Feb. 25**. *If you cannot submit your "creative way of presenting the book" in the discussion forum, describe it in the Forum and bring to class on March 3.*
		Respond to 2 postings

Chapter 5: Poetry,
Drama, and Humor
March 3
	1. After reading the chapter, identify and examine collections of poetry. Choose at least one poem from each of the following categories:
	  – A poem that tells a story
	  – A poem set to music (lyrics)
	  – A humorous poem
	  – A nonsense poem
	  – An inspirational poem
	  – A poem written especially for teenagers
	  – A named category of your choice.
	Then, produce a collection of your selected poetry, with a commentary for each, which addresses the potential appeal and value for young adults. Your collection will be evaluated based on presentation (organization, aesthetics, attribution), variety (breadth), and commentary (insightful perspective on the choices). You may submit your poetry collection and commentary as a catalog or booklet or in some other creative format on **March 5** by dropping the
		2+ books
		Respond to 2 postings on humorous books

collection off in my office. Be prepared to share a poem on **March 19**.

2. Select a humorous book (other than *Holes*), read it, and place it in its proper level in the Gentile and McMillen stages of interest (page 157). Document liberally from the book to justify your choice. Consider Table 5.1 on features of narrative humor as a possible guide. Submit to the Forum.

SPRING BREAK—
March 10

Time for more reading

Chapter 6: Adventure, Sports, Mysteries, and the Supernatural

March 17

1. Read an adventure book and apply the criteria presented in Table 6.1 (page 174). Provide a well-documented assessment with justifications of your impressions. Share in the Forum.

2 books

Respond to 2 postings
• 1 for an adventure
• 1 for a mystery

2. Select a YA Mystery and categorize it according to the Ocork scheme (pages 187–188). Then, review the novel for *viability* using the Waugh rules on pages (185–186). Share in the Forum.

3. Be prepared to share your selections in class.

Chapter 7: Fantasy, Science Fiction, Utopias and Dystopias

March 24

Choose one:

1. Read *The Giver*. Indicate which of the following quotes is most reflective of the novel. Write a paper that explores the quote and presents a rationale for your conclusion.

2 books

Respond to 2 postings
• 1 about *The Giver*
• 1 about the science fiction selection of a classmate

– *In fantasy, the imagined world is a global village. No action can take place in isolation. Every decision taken by the hero affects someone else, and sometimes the fate of the nation. It is a deeply social genre.* Jo-Anne Goodwin

– *The fantasy hero is not only a doer of deeds, but he also operates within a framework of morality. His compassion is as great as his courage – greater in fact. We might consider that his humane qualities, more than any other, are really what the hero is all about. I wonder if this reminds us of the best parts of our lives.* Lloyd Alexander

– *Fantasy, more than any other genre, is a literature of empowerment. In the real world, kids have little say. This is a given; it is the nature of childhood. In fantasy, however short, fat, unbeautiful, dreamy, or unlearned individuals may be, they find a realm in which those things are negated by strength. The catch—there is always a catch—is that empowerment brings trials.* Tamora Pierce.

(continued)

2. Read *The Giver.* Choose your own quotes from the book and write a paper that explores how these are significant in the book. Submit to the Forum.
Required:
3. Glean criteria for the evaluation of **science fiction** from the chapter. Select a book and apply these established criteria. Submit a paper delineating the criteria and discussing the literary merit of your selected novel.

Chapter 8: History and History Makers *March 31*	Choose one: 1. Read **both** *Esperanza Rising* **and** *Roll of Thunder, Hear My Cry.* Evaluate each as a work of historical fiction and discuss the merits and shortcomings of both in a *comparative analysis.* Submit via dropbox 2. Read **both** books. Then, choose one and prepare a **7-minute** overview of how you would introduce the <u>one</u> you chose to your classmates. Your presentation will be evaluated on succinctness of the overview, clarification of methodology, and aptness of motivational strategies you would use. You have creative license within the enforced 7-minute time limit.	2 books
Chapter 9: Nonfiction *April 7*	Group assignment: As per an assigned category of books, individually select two. In your group, prepare a presentation for the class which reflects your consideration of your selected books through the application of suggestions in Table 9.1 (page 259). Be sure to answer specific questions (listed below) related to the category. Each presentation is limited to **15 minutes**. • **Books about War**—Is the book interesting to read? If so, what makes it interesting: personal stories, good descriptions, drama of the situation, or other? Is there proof of authenticity? How did the writer get the information? Are there sources to consult for further information? What did the author or artist and layout designer do to make the book appeal to YAs? What is the tone? Does it glorify war or violence?	2 books from an assigned category

- **Books for Browsing**—Is this more than a book of trivia? Could students get interested in reading the whole book? Do you think such books merely increase tendencies of shortened attention spans? Where would you use such a book? Do you have faith in the information? Why or why not?
- **Information Books**—Is the topic likely to interest a wide range of YAs or is it specialized so that it would only be really important to a few kids, but irrelevant to most? Why? How should librarians balance the conflict? See if you have books in the group that fit into one of these areas: Current Events, Science and Technology, History from New Angles, Humanities and the Arts.
- **How-to Books**—What kind of information do YAs want to learn from books? In one library, how-to-draw books were the most popular nonfiction. Speculate on the reason(s). What frustrated you as a YA about these books? Are some of these books overly optimistic in showing YAs what they can do?
- **Books to Help Teens Learn Who They Are and How They Fit**—Is the focus on physical or emotional health? Does it combine the two? What aspects of emotional and mental health does it address? If it is a sex education book, is it fair to both genders? Would they both read the book or try to keep it a secret from the other gender? Would you say the book is appropriate for home use but not school use, vice-versa, or both? How does it differ from the books you read as a teenager?

Chapter 10: **Evaluating,** **Promoting, and** **Using Young Adult** **Books** *April 14*	1. Prepare a book talk for a **3–5 minute** presentation in class using guidelines in the chapter.	2–3 books and a magazine
	2. Locate and read a graphic novel. Submit your impressions on the Forum. Argue pro or con about its possible use in the classroom.	Respond to 2 postings
	3. Locate and examine a young adult magazine (e.g., Teen Vogue, Seventeen, Teen People). Submit your opinions about its possible use in your teaching.	

LAYER B

Chapter 11: Literature in the English Class: Short Stories, Novels, Creative Writing, Film and Thematic Units *April 21*	1. Develop a thematic unit on a book (or books) of choice. – Theme (an interesting title, rationale of interest for the students/classes, 3–5 goals – Support materials in annotated bibliography format (other books, short stories, poetry, nonfiction, other media) – Schedule of execution (including culminating activity) – Lesson planning (activities, any read-aloud sections, discussions and questions, writing and speaking activities) – Assessment includes a variety of well-sequenced, formative and summative assessments that are appropriate for the activities and the overall unit (e.g., sample rubrics and tests, plan for grading and evaluating — weights, percentages) – Evaluation will be based on overall presentation for clarity and completeness, attention to elements cited above, potential for stimulating interest in students, and quality of lesson planning, and feasibility of time frames suggested in the plan. 2. *Summarize* your unit in a one-page handout for class distribution and prepare a **5-minute** presentation to overview your plan during class on April 23.	0 book

LAYER A

Chapter 12: Censorship: Of Worrying and Wondering *April 28*	1. Prepare a rationale for teaching a book of choice. Review the text for guidelines in writing rationales. Submit to the Forum. 2. Select a title of choice from any genre. Write a review using the VOYA Evaluation Guide in Chapter 10. Rate the book accordingly, but defend your choices of *Quality* and *Popularity* with specific examples. Submit to the Forum. 3. Submit Book File (Make sure you follow the guidelines on page 2 of the syllabus. There should be 20 entries.)	1 or more books Respond to 2 postings

Layer C Rubric

Each assignment is worth 3 points; thus, assignments are graded on a 3 point scale.

Note: *There may be changes to this in the future because some assignments are obviously more involved. For example, the poetry assignment involves creating a collection of eight poems and critically evaluating each one, which is much more involved than listing five websites.)*

3 = good response, well developed, no mechanical and grammatical errors

2 = adequate response, but not well developed, may have some minor mechanical and grammatical errors

1 = minimal response, not well developed, several mechanical and grammatical errors

Layer B Rubric—Unit and Presentation

Each assignment is worth 5 points; thus, assignments are graded on a 5 point scale.

Add scores for Unit categories (A–E below; all but the *F. Presentation and Handout* category) and divide by 5 (categories) to get an average rating (between 1–5).

5 = Exemplary; 4 = Effective; 3 = Acceptable; 2 = Minimal; 1 = Unacceptable (something was submitted, but cannot be evaluated based on the criteria); 0 = not submitted.

	5 = Exemplary	4 = Effective	3 = Acceptable	2 = Minimal
A. Theme	Clear and creative theme; well written and complete rationale; includes 3–5 well written goals/ objectives	Clear and appropriate theme; well written rationale; includes 3–5 well written goals/ objectives	Has a clear theme; and a written rationale	A theme may be vaguely evident or written but is not at an appropriate level;

	5 = Exemplary	4 = Effective	3 = Acceptable	2 = Minimal
B. Support materials	Comprehensive, creative annotated bibliography written in appropriate form; includes a variety of interesting support materials	Complete list of support materials written in appropriate form and including at least 2–3 types of support materials	Moderate list of support materials, mostly written in annotated bibliographical form; includes more than one type of support material	A few support materials listed, but may not be in an annotated bibliography and/or may include only one type of support material
C. Schedule of execution	Clear and appropriate; shows a strong sense of timing	Clear; shows a good sense of timing	Includes a schedule; needs some improvement on timing activities	Schedule is vague and timing is evident, but may not be appropriate
D. Lesson Planning	Lesson plans are clear, creative, engaging, and consistently include quality higher order tasks and questions	Lesson plans are clear, engaging, and include quality higher order tasks and questions	Lesson plans are evident and somewhat engaging, and include some higher order tasks and questions	Lesson plans are evident, but weak and only minimally engaging. Higher order tasks and questions are either not included or it is difficult to discern whether or not they are included.
E. Assessment	Includes a variety of well-sequenced, formative and summative assessments that are appropriate for the activities and the overall unit	Includes a variety of formative and summative assessments for the activities and the overall unit	Includes assessments that generally provide data on student performance in the unit.	Includes some assessments, but they may not always focus on the key activities or the overall unit. They provide some data on student performance
F. Presentation and handout	Clear, focused, organized, shares key elements, interesting, and concise	Clear, focused, shares key elements, but not as interesting	Clear; may not be *as focused*, shares *some* key elements but may include extraneous elements	Has a handout about the unit, but neither the handout nor the presentation are clear or focused

Scoring: Add up points earned _____ divide by 6 = _____ Final score

Layer A Rubric—Rationale and VOYA Review

Each assignment is worth 5 points; thus, assignments are graded on a 5 point scale.

5 = Exemplary; 4 = Effective; 3 = Acceptable; 2 = Minimal; 1 = Unacceptable (something was submitted, but cannot be evaluated based on the criteria); 0 = not submitted.

	5 = Exemplary	4 = Effective	3 = Acceptable	2 = Minimal
Book Rationale	Clear, creative, complete, and well written rationale; virtually no grammatical and/or mechanical errors	Clear and appropriate theme; well written rationale; minimal grammatical and/or mechanical errors	Has a clearly written rationale, but the rationale could be more developed; some minor grammatical and/or mechanical errors	Has a written rationale that needs to be further developed; many minor or some major grammatical and/or mechanical errors
VOYA Review	Exceptionally well-written and well-justified review for both quality and popularity ratings; includes interesting details	Well-written and well-justified review for both quality and popularity ratings; includes interesting details	Written and somewhat justified review for both quality and popularity ratings; includes relevant details	Written but not well-justified for either or both quality and popularity ratings; includes few details

Each assignment is worth 5 points.

SUMMARY

In Chapter 5: *A Journey from Innocence to Experience—A Course in Young Adult Literature for Future Teachers,* middle and secondary teachers and university instructors were given a model for developing syllabi using a layered curriculum approach for a survey-type course. Within the layered curriculum, a variety of engaging activities and varied assessments were included. This chapter showed not only the scope of a course focused on differentiated instruction, but also the many ways that choice (and fun!) can be included in a university level course to ensure that all students are successful—**regardless of course level or student learning style.**

SUGGESTED READINGS

The books listed below are *some* of my favorites from when I took the YA Literature course. Of course, there are many honor and award books (e.g., Newbery, Coretta Scott King, Michael Printz) that should be read. There are lists available on the web and books available in bookstores, specifically focusing on books for teens (e.g., Anita Silvey's (2006) *500 Great Books for Teens*).

Adventure

Avi. The True Confessions of Charlotte Doyle

Fantasy/Science Fiction/Utopias and Dystopias

Farmer, Nancy. *The House of Scorpion*
Haddix, Margaret Peterson. *Among the Hidden*
Lowry, Lois. *The Giver*
Lowry, Lois. *Gathering Blue*
Lowry, Lois. *The Messenger*
Pulliam, Phillip. *The Gold Compass*
Slade, Arthur. *Dust*

Historical Fiction

Curtis, Christopher Paul. *Bud, Not Buddy.*
Cushman, Karen. *The Midwife's Apprentice*
Filipovic, Zlata. *Zlata's Diary.*
Jiang, Ji Li. *Red Scarf Girl: A Memoir of the Cultural Revolution*
Spiegelman, Art. *Maus I* (a graphic novel)
Spiegelman, Art. *Maus II* (a graphic novel)

Humor

Mackler, Carolyn. The Earth, My Butt, and Other Big Round Things
Philbrick, Rodman. *Freak the Mighty*
Wolff, Virginia, Euwer. *Make Lemonade*

Realistic Fiction

Blume, Judy. *Forever*
Brashares, Ann. *Sisterhood of the Traveling Pants*
Codell, Esme' Raji. *Sahara Special*
Cormier, Robert. *The Chocolate War*
Dessen, Sarah. *That Summer*
Draper, Sharon. *Tears of A Tiger*
Draper, Sharon. *Forged by Fire*
Frank, E.R. *Friction*
Hinton, S.E. *Rumble Fish*
Hinton, S.E. *That Was Then, This Is Now*
Hinton, S.E. *The Outsiders*
Meyers, Walter Dean. *Monster*
Zindel, Paul. *The Pigman*

Mystery

Christie, Agatha. *And Then There Were None*
Cormier, Robert. *I am the Cheese*
Cormier, Robert. *The Rag and Bone Shop*
Glenn, Mel. *Who Killed Mr. Chippendale?*
Raskin, Ellen. *The Westing Game.*

Non-Fiction

Covey, Sean. *The 6 Most Important Decisions You'll Ever Make.*
Covey, Sean. *The 7 Habits of Highly Effective Teens.*
Johnson, Spencer. *Who Moved My Cheese? For Teens*
Paul, Anthea. *Girlosophy: A Soul Survival Kit.*
Schroder, Barbara and Wiatt, Carrie. *The Diet For Teenagers Only.*

CHAPTER 6

CONVINCE ME

A Syllabus for a Freshman Composition Course Focused on Writing Arguments

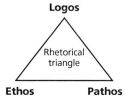

Logos

Rhetorical triangle

Ethos   Pathos

The Perfect Norm, pages 117–142
Copyright © 2009 by Information Age Publishing
All rights of reproduction in any form reserved.

INTRODUCTION

Nearly one decade into the twenty-first century, a "Framework for 21st Century Learning" (2007, www.21stcenturyskills.org) has been developed by a partnership consisting of member organizations as diverse as Ford Motor Company, The National Education Association, McGraw-Hill, Apple, and The Corporation for Public Broadcasting. This group feels high-school graduates (and, of course, college graduates) must have attained the following thinking and learning attributes to be considered "future-ready":

- Exercising sound reasoning in understanding
- Making complex choices
- Framing, analyzing, and solving problems
- Demonstrating originality and inventiveness in work
- Developing, implementing, and communicating new ideas to others
- Being open and responsive to new and diverse perspectives.

These are not your grandmother's-generation thinking and work skills, nor can they be taught with twentieth-century teacher-centered pedagogy, nor can they be substantively assessed using standardized multiple-choice tests. The twenty-first century high school and college graduate must be prepared with a set of skills, knowledge, and dispositions that will help them successfully navigate increasingly complex work environments which feature an over-abundance of information and rapid changes in technology. These graduates will be asked to collaborate with people from different cultures and backgrounds in a spirit of mutual respect at a level heretofore unprecedented, not just because of our increasingly diverse society, but also because of the impact of globalization (the "world is flat" concept of Friedman). And, they must be prepared to take on and succeed in jobs that have not yet been invented.

To prepare these future-ready graduates, teachers must also be future-ready, i.e., they must assume new roles and abandon unproductive, ineffective methods and beliefs. Our own state of North Carolina is one among others that have aligned professional teaching standards with the 21st Century Learning Framework mentioned above. Excerpts from the new, soon-to-take-effect Professional Teaching Standards vision statement (2008, www.ncptsc.org) illustrate how the State aims to operationalize 21st century learning (highlights added below for emphasis):

- **Teachers can no longer cover material; they, along with their students, uncover solutions**. They teach existing core content that is revised to include critical thinking, problem solving, and information and communications technology (ICT) literacy. [Note: In other words, teachers need to ensure students accumulate a body of knowledge sufficient for them to be able to make sense of isolated facts and new knowledge that comes their way, but students should not be expected to memorize endless facts. Teachers need not, and should not, present all foundational knowledge via lecture. In fact, lecturing is the **least** "brain-friendly" teaching strategy an educator can employ.]

- **Teachers make the content they teach engaging, relevant, and meaningful** to students' lives. [Note: Students need to know, and deserve to know, the purpose and usefulness of what they are asked to learn.]
- In their classrooms, teachers facilitate instruction, encouraging all students to use 21st century skills so [students can] **discover how to learn, innovate, collaborate, and communicate their ideas**.
- Teachers include **assessments that are authentic and structured and demonstrate student understanding**. [Note: In other words, allow students to demonstrate their understanding in a variety if meaningful ways.]

While industry, government, and educational institutions have historically formed alliances that have tinkered with curriculum, the zeitgeist of the twenty-first century presents us with a sense of urgency akin to the Sputnik era, when the government/education/industry alliance made substantive, rather than incremental, revisions to curriculum and educational priorities. Today, we have even a greater sense of urgency than in the Sputnik era because of the rapid, even frenzied, speed at which new information is generated. Global threats to the environment, worldwide competition's affect on employment opportunities and our economy, plus exponential technological innovation are key indicators that tell us **mere** evolutionary changes in curriculum and educational practices are insufficient. We must truly put teeth in mission statements like North Carolina's: "Every public school student will graduate from high school, globally competitive for work and prepared for life in the 21st century" (www.ncptsc.org). To tinker around the edges of curriculum, rather than make foundational changes about how students learn and teachers teach, would be hypocritical. Even worse, it would perpetuate a disconnect between the ostensible, **hopeful claims** of the average school system (even in the current *No Child Left Behind* climate, schools claim to "educate all students") and **the reality** of absolute, unthinking, authoritative impositions of mile-wide, inch-deep curriculum and zero-sum-game standardized assessment.

From our perspective, while significant changes need to be made—in how we teach, in how students are allowed to learn and express learning, and in how new teachers are trained—it is really a matter of finally implementing what research has already taught us: that "brain-friendly," culturally responsive, differentiated strategies are perfectly uited to teaching and learning 21st century skills. Thus, significant reform need not start from scratch.

REVIEW OF THE UNIT

The syllabus that follows was developed for a freshman composition course at a university. Its focus is on effective argument, but it also features skill building in the documentation of research, writing style, and editing/proofreading. Since freshmen in college are not far removed in age or writing experience from seniors (or even juniors) in high school, this syllabus could easily be adapted to a high school curriculum as a writing unit. From my experience as a university-level teacher of composition, the quality of writing among students is far below the standard demanded in twenty-first century jobs. We teachers may spend energy on bemoaning this state of affairs and cry shame that young people don't read enough or that they spend too much time massacring the language with each text-message. However, a better focus for our energies is to dig in and do something about it. We know that writing and speaking well opens doors for our students, and the failure to exhibit effective communication skills (literacy) closes those doors. We know that young people like to argue, and we also know that their concept of arguing—which foregrounds emotion, mostly anger, and often ignores facts, reason, and logic—is far removed from the effective kinds of argument that the real world demands, e.g., the reasoned debate of a courtroom, the cool-headed logic of a business negotiation, the fair-minded mutuality inherent in a diplomatic proposal, or the multiple perspectives necessary for an effective critical review of an institution or a work of art. Thus, since teachers must invest lots of effort when they take on the task of helping students acquire and perfect writing skills, they might as well double the payoff of their investment by teaching effective rhetoric alongside effective style and correctness. Differentiation, in the form of "brain-friendly" and culturally responsive strategies, is the key to accomplishing this Herculean task.

Since all good planning should begin with an eye toward assessment, I began developing this syllabus by listing the student learning outcomes I would be evaluating. Before I could write them, however, I had to decide upon the content I wanted to teach and then divide it into four categories: (a) effective style, (b) rhetoric/argument, (c) documentation, and (d) usage/punctuation/correctness. I then fleshed out each category, listing the topics I planned to cover and the knowledge/skills I planned to assess. I ended up with the following:

Category 1: Effective Style

- Define stylistic elements, (e.g., coherence, unity, emphasis, clarity, conciseness)
- Practice strategies that achieve key elements, i.e., using parallel construction, using transitions, repeating key words, employing subordination and coordination techniques (e.g., embedding, cumulative sentences)

Category 2: Rhetoric/Argument

- How to think about an issue for formal argument: Definition, Context, Description, Evaluation
- Definitions of *logos, pathos,* and *ethos*; how to recognize them in popular discourse
- Definitions of the logical fallacies; how to recognize them in popular discourse; the ethical and rhetorical implications of using them
- Analysis of arguments

Category 3: Documentation (and Avoiding Plagiarism)

- Rules for using quotation marks
- Defining *paraphrase, direct quote,* and *summary*; recognizing examples of each in published writing and writing original examples to avoid plagiarism
- Practicing MLA and APA styles of citation and documentation

Category 4: Usage/Punctuation/Correctness

- Review uses of all punctuation with an emphasis on specialty punctuation: semicolons, colons, hyphens, dashes, parentheses, brackets, ellipsis; practice using them
- Review twenty most common usage errors in student writing; practice recognizing and correcting them.

After listing what I wanted to cover within the curriculum/syllabus, my next task was to weight each category (or sub-unit) as a percent of the final grade for the course. Since **rhetoric/argument** and **documentation** involved lots of new content and skill building for my students, I weighted them heavier than the **usage/punctuation/correctness** and **effective style** sub-units, which focused mostly on a review of prior knowledge. In the end, the points for each unit were as follows:

Rhetoric/Argument	200 points
Documentation	100
Effective Style	60
Usage/Punctuation/Correctness	40
Course Total	400 points

The points converted to letter grades as follows:

344–400 = A	(90–100%)
285–343 = B	(80–89%)
224–284 = C	(70–79%)
160–223 = D	(60–69%)
159–0 = F	(59% and below)

Within each sub-unit I followed the advice of Kathie Nunley in *Layered Curriculum* (2004) and gave students **lots of choice** by assigning points to a number of "brain-friendly" activities from which students could choose to demonstrate their knowledge. Generally, I assigned fewer points to activities which provided students with the opportunity to gain a general understanding of subject matter. Nunley calls these "Layer C" activities because a student cannot earn higher than a C grade by completing them. I assigned more points (weight) to "Layer B" activities (in which students are asked to manipulate knowledge learned in Layer C) and "Layer A" activities (which involve the most complex thinking among the layered activities—those that ask students to apply knowledge and skills learned in layers C and B to current events and real-world, **authentic** situations and to form an opinion and/or take an ethical stance on a controversial issue and defend that opinion).

After assigning points to sub-units, I was ready to brainstorm—sometimes by myself and sometimes in consultation with colleagues—about activities that would engage students in the subject matter and offer students some choice in how they could demonstrate learning and practice skill building. I was guided by the principles of differentiated instruction, culturally responsive pedagogy, and "brain-friendly" research as I developed a range of activities which would allow students to **choose** the ways they would feel most comfortable demonstrating their understanding of content and improving their skills. Both Nunley (2004) and Tate (2003, 2004) were useful references, spurring my creativity in developing a variety of engaging activities. All in all, my activities comprised 16 out of the 20 brain-friendly teaching strategies outlined by Tate—reciprocal teaching, role playing, games, mnemonic devices, metaphors and similes, to name a few—all in just one syllabus. The activities, their assigned points, and their place in the overall curriculum are outlined below, just as I presented it on the syllabus.

The final step involved developing rubrics for each **kind** of B and A Layer activity and including them on the syllabus so that students knew, up front, what they had to do to earn the required points on products and performances that earned them a good grade. By the way, it should be noted that the philosophy which underlies Nunley's *Layered Curriculum* is opposed to granting grades to students for merely finishing a project, activity, or performance. She would liken this to rewarding busy work rather than assessing what was **actually learned**. What Nunley argues is that activities which students choose to complete are only the ways students choose to learn and practice particular knowledge, skills, and dispositions. They are required to complete a number of activities which add up to a prescribed number of points because they need to have several encounters with material in order to have a deep understanding of it. Summative assessment is a separate issue, involving not just the completion of a product, but rather the demonstration of mastery over the subject matter represented in the product. This mastery is often a matter of a student's answering on-the-spot questions about the subject matter at a *proficient* (80%+) or *accomplished* (90%+) level on C-Layer activities. Mastery at B and A layers means the product produced meets the description of either *exemplary, effective*, or *acceptable* on specific rubrics.

I have outlined my planning process to demonstrate the confluence of perspectives required for planning a curriculum which features differentiated instruction and which honors principles of culturally relevant pedagogy and the findings of neuro-cognitive ("brain-friendly") research. I have found that the investment of time, up front, yields dramatic results when I implement. Students—once they acclimate to an academic environment which features **choice** and which requires them to be responsible for their learning—are more engaged, curious, on-task, focused, and self-motivated than in non-differentiated classrooms. On the other hand, I (the teacher) am not forced to spend my time disciplining or trying to motivate students to pay attention. I no longer **fight** student inclinations; rather, they **invite** me to coach, comment, facilitate, join them on their learning journey. What a great way to spend one's teaching day.

THE UNIT/SYLLABUS

SYLLABUS—Composition I

Office: xxx Communications Building   ENG 1110
Office Hours: TR 8:00–9:25; 10:45–1:00; 2:15–4:00   TR 1:00–2:15 pm
E-mail: xxxx@nccu.edu   200 COM
Office Phone: 530-xxxx

NCCU School of Education Conceptual Framework: Preparing Educators for Diverse Cultural Contexts

Catalog Description:

ENG 1110. English Composition I (3) A study of the essentials of English composition and rhetoric, with emphasis on expository essays.

Course Description

This course is designed to help students develop a wide variety of process-oriented writing skills and strategies. You will learn about how to improve your own writing skills, particularly how to argue/persuade effectively and convincingly. You will also practice giving meaningful peer feedback, self-assessment of your own writing, and how to avoid unwitting plagiarism. In order to complete this course successfully, you will need to reflect upon your own writing practices, skills, and attitudes; study and practice the elements of effective persuasive writing; and demonstrate responsibility (including attending classes, practicing the steps of the writing process; submitting papers on deadline and researching the advice of professional writers and writing teachers).

The course will cover a range of skills and activities all designed to complement each other and to build your understanding of what constitutes effective writing in general, and effective persuasive writing in particular. The student learning outcomes listed below are ambitious, but achievable, only if you commit to the course. That commitment means that you attend all class sessions (exceptions: emergencies and written excuses from a doctor or University authority). During each class session, we will introduce ideas and practice techniques that will develop your writing and peer response skills. If you miss them, there will be gaps in your knowledge. While readings will be assigned, much of the class work will involve mini-lectures and many self-chosen participatory activities. The experience of participating in these activities with peers is a significant part of the learning in this course; as such, they are impossible to make up in their original form. If you are absent, you are still responsible for the work missed; therefore, obtain notes from a fellow student, see me, or consult the course web site for handouts.

Subject matter you will write about will largely derive from your own experience, either as memories or from deliberate observation, reading, and research. Assignments will ask you to practice the key steps of the writing process—prewriting, writing, revising, and proofreading. Issues of style, grammar, usage, and principles of composition will be interwoven into whole-class discussion and small-group activities, using your writing products and those of other students as examples. In short, you will learn about writing principally **by doing a lot of writing** and by analyzing and talking about your own and others' writing.

Supplementary Texts:

Lunsford, Andrea A. & John J. Ruszkiewicz. *Everything's an Argument*. Boston, MA: Bedford/ St. Martin's, 1999.

O'Conner, Patricia.T. *Woe Is I: The Grammarphobe's Guide to Better English in Plain English*. New York: Riverhead Books, 2003.

Truss, Lynne. *Eats, Shoots and Leaves: The Zero Tolerance Approach to Punctuation*. New York: Gotham Books, 2003.

Collegiate handbooks, dictionaries, and a thesaurus.

Student Leaning Outcomes:

- After participating in class mini-lectures, reviewing writing models, researching on the Internet and/or a variety of texts, and practicing techniques in class, students will write out-of-class and in-class pieces which demonstrate competence in writing style, effective use of rhetorical strategies, and mastery in the use of the conventions of Edited American English (EAE).
- Given in-class individual and group activities on writing techniques and issues of correctness, students will demonstrate mastery through quizzes and oral defense of their work.
- After taking notes on mini-lectures and reflecting on book chapters and articles on rhetorical strategies and techniques, students will demonstrate understanding by developing individual and small-group products.
- In the process of responding to the variety of assigned readings, students will complete informal writing assignments, including journal entries, reflections, and free-writes.
- By reviewing the conventions of Standard English usage and punctuation in professional writing, given instruction in strategies for revision, and by preparing a variety of self-chosen products, students

will practice revising, proofreading, and editing for clarity and mechanical correctness.

- After reading texts on usage, argument, and correctness, students will reflect upon their own strengths and/or limitations as writers of arguments.
- By using the Blackboard online course environment for this course and the Internet, students will incorporate various forms of electronic media and technology in daily class activities, including online research, discussion, and preparation of assignments.
- By attending to issues of correctness (usage and punctuation) through a variety of activities, students will develop a checklist of common errors to consult when revising and proofreading; in addition, they will work to develop a "zero tolerance" for surface errors by submitting increasingly "perfected" (i.e., with virtually no surface errors) writing products as the course progresses.

Note: This syllabus and schedule are subject to change depending upon the needs of the class.

Class Policies:

Journals. Journals will be used to encourage ongoing reflection on what you are learning as you progress through the course. The natural subject for the journal entries will be your reactions to readings in *Woe Is I; Eats, Shoots and Leaves;* and *Everything's an Argument.* However, your reactions to activities you perform in class, plus your reactions to writing and argumentation issues encountered in outside research on the Internet, are also appropriate subjects to reflect upon.

Class Attendance/Participation. Class attendance is critical to your overall success in this course. Missing sessions will leave a gap in your knowledge and will slow your progress in further developing your writing. Class time will be devoted to mini-lectures, practicing writing techniques, and group activities which will guide your writing development. Your participation in class activities will help develop your ability to collaborate and willingness to entertain the ideas of others. Once attendance is taken, you will be responsible for reminding the instructor that you made it to class.

I expect you to attend all classes and to be on time. If you miss two classes (a week of class for a Tuesday/Thursday course), expect your final grade to suffer. If you miss four classes (two weeks of class), I am required by the University to drop you from the class with an NF for non-attendance, a policy I will not hesitate to enforce. Please be aware of the fact that the University makes no distinction between excused and unexcused absences—an absence is an absence. I take the roll in the first five minutes of class. If you are on time, you will not be marked absent. For every three times you are tardy (late to class), you will be assessed one absence.

Courtesy. Please treat all members of this class with the same respect and dignity you want for yourself. You should strive for excellence and improvement in all aspects of your work. As your teacher, I pledge that I will treat you with respect; I will judge your work fairly; I will work hard to help you learn to improve your thinking and writing skills. My goal for this class is to see you leave this course as stronger and more confident writers. Your success will be up to you.

In addition, **please turn off all cell phones before you enter the classroom**. Phones that ring will be answered by the instructor; phones that ring more than once will be taken by the instructor and held until the end of class. Unless it is a real emergency, do not excuse yourself from class to take a phone call. It is discourteous to do so because it implies that your casual phone calls are more important than your learning in this class.

Please come to class on time. I do not accept the excuse that you were late to class because the elevators were busy or slow or full. Use the stairs! If you know ahead of time that you will be late to class or miss class altogether, please give me the courtesy of emailing or calling me to let me know.

Accommodations. Students requiring accommodations or with accessibility concerns should contact the Office of Student Support Services at 530-6325 and inform the instructor.

Evaluation. Students will be assessed both formatively and summatively. Formative evaluation will include written and verbal comments on submitted assignments, class discussion of products you produce, and mastery quizzes. The **midterm** grade will be determined by the points earned for completed products and quizzes. The **final** grade will comprise points earned on all required products and grades on quizzes/oral defense of your work products.

Rhetoric/Argument	200 points
Documentation	100
Effective Style	60
Usage/Punctuation/Correctness	40
Course Total	400 points

The points converted to letter grades as follows:

344–400 = A
285–343 = B
224–284 = C
160–223 = D
159–0 = F

Deadlines. Unless stated otherwise, all papers/products are due as indicated on the syllabus. Do not use the day papers are due as a time to miss class. **Type your papers before class time, not during.** I do not accept late papers or culminating projects. I provide plenty of time and notice for your assignments, so don't make the mistake of waiting until the last minute to begin your work. If you are having trouble with an assignment, you usually know well before the due date, so contact me early about any problems you're having.

Major products are due at the beginning of class on their due dates. I take roll in the first five minutes of class, so I expect you to be in your seat and ready to begin. This rule is especially important on the day a major product is due. If you come to class six minutes late on the day a major product is due, I will not accept it, and you will receive a zero for the assignment.

Computer problems are epidemic on campus (this includes computer viruses, broken printers, malfunctioning disk drives, and incompatible software programs). Consider this as a warning and protect yourself from needless heartache and pain. For your own peace of mind, save copies (both diskette and paper) of all your written work. Your preparation should always include a handwritten draft or notes. If you compose at the keyboard, print out each version when you leave the computer. Don't wait until the last minute to complete or print your papers. Don't rely on a single diskette or jump-drive for all your writing, for it can easily be lost, stolen, or broken. I do not accept computer mishaps as an excuse for incomplete, late, or missing work. Late work will receive a zero.

Honor Code. Participation in this course includes the requirement that all work will be original. Any breach of the University's Honor Code strikes at the ideals of academic honesty and responsible citizenship that are the hallmarks of this university. We will review briefly the specific conventions regarding paper submission, documentation, and plagiarism. Be advised that plagiarism is a serious violation of North Carolina Central University's Honor Code. Any paper that contains plagiarized work will receive a zero (0). I will not tolerate academic dishonesty. Please review the consequences of and due process procedures for Honor Code violations in the student handbook.

Conferences. I am always available for consultation about your written assignments, so please make an appointment if you would like some help. I encourage you to see me if you're having any difficulties with a specific assignment. My door is always open, so please take advantage of my willingness to help you achieve your best.

Quizzes and Oral Defense. These are used to determine your mastery of course material. They occur shortly after you have completed and submitted self-chosen products for each mini-unit in the course. You cannot earn a final grade by merely submitting the required number of products. You earn a final grade by demonstrating that you have learned the material (i.e., techniques of argument, effective style, the conventions of Edited American English) at a mastery level (minimum 80% correct) on the quizzes and oral defenses.

COURSE CALENDAR

EFFECTIVE STYLE
LAYER C

Weeks 1–4 1/5–1/30	Complete the required journal assignment and choose 10 points from each group (1–3) for a total of 30 points	Points earned
Complete assignments in any order, but do not wait until the end of week four to submit them.	**Required** Read *Woe Is I* and write one reflection (minimum ½ page) for each of its eleven chapters in a journal. Your reflection should include your response to the subject matter covered. What did you learn that was new? How will you remember to use your new knowledge?	10
Note: Expect an oral or written quiz (sometimes, an oral defense) to be asked of you by the instructor after you have completed all your chosen activities from each group.	**Group One** • Consult 3 different college handbooks; write definitions and provide 2 examples for each of the following elements of style: coherence, unity, emphasis, clarity, conciseness (concision).	5
	• Make flash cards which define each of the following elements of style and provide 2 examples for each: coherence, unity, emphasis, clarity, conciseness (concision).	5
Consider your completion of these activities as your way of learning about the subject matter at hand and of studying for your quiz.	• Describe the following elements of style as if they were heroic characters in a comic book: coherence, unity, emphasis, clarity, conciseness (concision). Describe how they would act, how they would "save" a piece of writing, what their characteristics are. Include a cartoon drawing of each character.	5
	• Teach the following elements of style—coherence, unity, emphasis, clarity, conciseness (concision)—to at least one classmate; prepare a test to determine what he/she learned.	10
	Group Two • Combine several groups of sentences on a handout supplied by the instructor, using techniques of subordination and coordination.	5
	• Take notes on a mini-lecture about techniques for coordination and subordination, e.g., embedding relative clauses, reducing independent clauses to phrases or words, using conjunctive adverbs to connect related sentences. Participate in a practice session at the blackboard.	5

- Read about sentence combining in 3 different college   5
  handbooks; then, write the techniques in your own words
  and write 10 examples of using the techniques in your
  course notebook.

- Create an easy game for fellow students to play. The   5
  object of the game should be to create effective sentences
  which properly use techniques of subordination and
  coordination. Write the rules for the game and ask two
  peers to play it.

Group Three

- With a partner, design and display a poster which defines   5
  parallel construction and then illustrate it with 2 examples
  each using single-word adjectives, gerund phrases,
  prepositional phrases, dependent clauses, and participles.
  Share with peers.

- Create a PowerPoint presentation for your peers that   5
  defines parallel construction and provides 2 examples
  each using single-word adjectives, gerund phrases,
  prepositional phrases, dependent clauses, and participles.
  Show it to peers.

- Create a manipulative which allows a peer to play with   5
  sentence elements to create parallel construction using
  single-word adjectives, gerund phrases, prepositional phrases,
  dependent clauses, and participles. Play it with peers.

- Access an interactive grammar program on the Internet   5
  and complete at least 20 questions on parallel construction.
  Keep testing until you achieve at least 90% mastery.

LAYER B

Week 4	Choose and complete one of the following activities	Points earned
Begin this assignment only AFTER you have completed and been tested on all chosen Layer C activities. This assignment will be evaluated according to a rubric which is attached to this syllabus. Due: 1/30	• Analyze the essays of 2 different writers in *Newsweek* or *TIME*. Highlight examples of coordination and subordination techniques used by each writer. Write a description of each writer's style based on the kinds of techniques they each tend to use.	10
	• Locate 4 different pieces of writing, each intended for a different audience. Briefly describe each style, based on the kinds of coordination and subordination techniques used, and the style's affect on readers based on the techniques used most often.	10
	• Analyze an essay you have written for another course. Describe your style, based on the kinds of coordination and subordination techniques you use. If you find you do not use these techniques very often or very well in the piece of writing you analyze, re-write the essay to include these techniques. Highlight the changes you made form the original and attach a copy of the original.	10

LAYER A

Week 5	Choose and complete one of the following activities	**Points earned**
Due: 2/2	• Read one article each in a politically conservative and in a politically liberal magazine. Describe differences and similarities you see in their respective styles of writing.	10
	• Locate a Web site for a university in England, Israel, and India. Describe differences and similarities you see in the respective styles of writing on each Web site.	10

RHETORIC/ARGUMENT
LAYER C

Weeks 5–8 2/2–2/27	Complete the required assignment and then choose any combination of activities which add up to 60 points	**Points earned**
Complete assignments in any order, but do not wait until the end of week eight to submit them. Note: Expect an oral or written quiz (sometimes, an oral defense) to be asked of you by the instructor after you have completed all your chosen activities from each group. Consider your completion of these activities as your way of learning about the subject matter at hand and of studying for your quiz.	**Required** Read *Everything's an Argument* and write one reflection (minimum ½ page) for each of its chapters in a journal. Your reflection should include your response to the subject matter covered. What did you learn that was new? How will you remember to use your new knowledge?	40
	• Read one article in two of the following types of magazine: business, sports, fashion, cooking, or politics. Write a brief summary of the claim being made in each article and the main reasons (warrants) used to support the claim. Attach the articles to your summaries and highlight/ label instances of logos, ethos, and pathos in the articles.	15
	• Listen and take notes on a mini-lecture about argument, logos, ethos, pathos, logical fallacies, warrants, claim.	15
	• Make one or more Foldables® which include definitions for and examples of logos, ethos, pathos, all the logical fallacies, warrants, claim. Consult the instructor's display of various Foldables® in the back of the room. For more information about Foldables®, Google Dinah Zike (the creator) or the word *Foldables*.	10
	• Make a collage using words and pictures from advertisements for cigarettes, a particular brand of liquor, a particular model of car, or a particular label of clothing; attach a written summary of how many times the ads appeal to logos, pathos, and ethos and whether logical fallacies were used to persuade potential buyers. Speculate on what audience the ad is aiming to reach.	10
	• Construct a board game, with written rules, that teaches your peers the definitions of ethos, logos, pathos, warrants, claims, and the logical fallacies and which teaches your peers to recognize them. Ask 2 or 3 classmates to play the game.	15

- Watch a political comedian (video or tv appearance). Write down the examples of logos, pathos, and ethos used to make the humorous points. Also include any logical fallacies used. What are the claim and warrants used? 20

- Field trip: Go to a political rally or to a political headquarters office. Gather literature and take notes on 1–2 interviews you have with advocates for the particular candidate running for office. What rhetorical devices (of logos, ethos, pathos, logical fallacies) do you find? Highlight them on the literature and on your interview notes. Be prepared to share. 10

- Role play: Pretend you are an investigative reporter who is going to interview someone who advocates for a cause (e.g., a lobbyist for tobacco companies or constituents interested in saving the environment). Write a series of questions you'd ask in order to determine what the advocate wants to persuade a congressman to do for his/her cause, what reasons support the argument, what techniques of persuasion he/she will use to persuade the congressman to act in favor of the cause. Note: To prepare your questions, locate a blog for that cause on the Internet. Copy it and highlight instances of logos, ethos, pathos, logical fallacies. Look for the claim and reasons. 15

- Write a poem or lyrics for a song or rap which includes definitions and examples of logos, ethos, pathos, all the logical fallacies, warrant, claims. Perform your poem/rap/ song for classmates. 20

- Draw a cartoon that includes characters representing logos, ethos, pathos, logical fallacies. Create a storyline in which these characters interact by trying to persuade each other (or a reader) about something.

LAYER B

Week 8	Choose and complete one of the following activities	Points earned
Begin this assignment only AFTER you have completed and been tested on all chosen Layer C activities.	• If you could make an argument machine, how would it look? What features would it contain? How would you persuade someone to buy it? What is the best audience for this machine (demographics and psychographics)? Write an essay which includes an illustration, or create a 3D mockup with labels and present the machine in an oral presentation to the class.	50
This assignment will be evaluated according to a rubric which is attached to this syllabus. Due: 2/27	• Who, in your opinion, are the more effective arguers— males or females? Defend your belief in a well-written persuasive essay, in a PowerPoint presentation, or in a debate with a fellow classmate in which one of you argues for males and one of you argues for females. Present your arguments to the class.	50

LAYER A

Week 9	Choose and complete one of the following activities	Points earned
Due: 3/2	• Is FOX News as "fair and balanced" as they advertise? Take a position and defend it in a well-written persuasive essay which effectively uses the rhetorical devices and stylistic techniques we have studied so far in this course.	50
	• The United States is ready for a woman or African American President. Take a position and defend it in a well-written persuasive essay which effectively uses the rhetorical devices and stylistic techniques we have studied so far in this course.	50

DOCUMENTATION
LAYER C

Weeks 9–11 3/2–3/20	Complete the required assignments and then choose any combination of activities which add up to 40 points	Points earned
Complete assignments in any order, but do not wait until the end of week eleven to submit them. Note: Expect an oral or written quiz (sometimes, an oral defense) to be asked of you by the instructor after you have completed all your chosen activities from each group. Consider your completion of these activities as your way of learning about the subject matter at hand and of studying for your quiz.	**Required** Read *Eats, Shoots and Leaves** and write one reflection (minimum ½ page) for each of its chapters in a journal. Your reflection should include your response to the subject matter covered. What did you learn that was new? How will you remember to use your new knowledge?	20
	• Listen and take notes on a mini-lecture and demonstration about how to use quotation marks in relation to other kinds of punctuation and how to format direct quotations. Also included are the differences between direct quotes, paraphrase, and summary—and how to avoid plagiarism.	10
	• Locate an article in a discipline-specific journal. Highlight and label direct quotations, paraphrases, and summary statements.	10
	• Make flashcards which define paraphrase, direct quotation, and summary statement. Study them with a partner.	10
	• With a partner, draw a poster or make a Foldables® which illustrates how to avoid plagiarism by citing quotations, paraphrases, and summary statements properly.	10
	• With a partner, create and present a PowerPoint about to avoid plagiarism by citing quotations, paraphrases, and summary statements properly.	10
	• Design and illustrate a children's book on how to properly use citations with quotes, paraphrases, and summary statements.	10
	• Write a song or rap lyric that outlines the direct and indirect ways students plagiarize. End the song by referring to the consequences for plagiarism from the University Catalog.	10

- Teach 2 classmates how to set up a Works Cited Page using   10
  MLA and APA formats. Create a quiz on the subject matter
  and administer it to the classmates you taught.
- Make a poster or Foldables® comparing MLA and APA   10
  Works Cited Page entries for a single author of a book, an
  article in an edited collection, an article in a journal, and
  a World Wide Web site.

---

* Note: I am including the reading of *Eats, Shoots and Leaves* in Unit 3 rather than Unit 4
because I want students to be familiar with punctuation rules **before** tackling the last unit.
Additionally, since students will be writing their culminating essay in Unit 4, I wanted them
to be able to focus on the argument without having also to learn initially about specialty
punctuation at the same time.

LAYER B

Week 11	Choose and complete one of the following activities	Points earned
Begin this assignment only AFTER you have completed and been tested on all chosen Layer C activities.	• Interview 3 teachers to find out if and how they detect plagiarism. What do they think should be the consequences for plagiarism and why? Write a well-written essay, using all the knowledge you have learned thus far in the previous 2 units, to summarize your interviews and end the essay with your own thoughts about why you should not plagiarize.	20
This assignment will be evaluated according to a rubric which is attached to this syllabus. Due: 3/20	• Create a plagiarized essay and submit it to Google.com. Copy the source(s) from which the essay was plagiarized and highlight the offending parts on both the sources and the essay. Then write an essay which outlines what you found and what you learned from this investigative exercise.	20

Spring Break from March 21 through March 29

LAYER A

Week 12	Choose and complete one of the following activities	Points earned
Due: 3/30	Defend or refute one of the following propositions in a well-written essay using all the knowledge you have learned about writing style, argument, and documentation in this course. Use at least 2 sources as evidence in your essay and include a Works Cited Page in either APA or MLA format:	
	• If you don't get caught, it is okay to plagiarize.	20
	• Politicians (or advertisers) principally use logical fallacies to persuade.	20

USAGE, PUNCTUATION, CORRECTNESS
LAYER C

Weeks 13–15 **3/30–4/17**	Choose any combination of activities which add up to 5 points for Group One and 10 points for Group Two	**Points** **earned**
Complete assignments in any order, but do not wait until the end of week fifteen to submit them. Note: Expect an oral or written quiz (sometimes, an oral defense) to be asked of you by the instructor after you have completed all your chosen activities from each group. Consider your completion of these activities as your way of learning about the subject matter at hand and of studying for your quiz.	**Required** Take a pre-test on the 20 common usage and mechanical errors of writers. Make an error log of the ones you missed. **Group One** • Look up the rules of items you missed in two different college handbooks. Write the rules in your own words and provide examples of how to correct each error. • Review 2 papers (or first drafts) you wrote in other courses. Highlight any errors in them that match the errors listed in your error log. Then, fix the errors on your papers. • Make flashcards, a poster, or a Foldables® that illustrates and lists the rules for correcting all 20 common usage and mechanical errors. • Develop a mnemonic device, poem, or rap lyric for remembering how to correct the 20 common usage and mechanical errors. **Group Two** • Portray 10 different kinds of punctuation as cartoon characters. Label each character with descriptions of their specialized characteristics. How does each function in the world of writing? How do they act in relation to each other? • Make up a song or poem that explains how to use 10 kinds of punctuation correctly. Perform it for your classmates. • Write 20 original sentences using 10 kinds of punctuation correctly. Be prepared to defend your choices by citing the rules for proper use. • Review the definitions and some examples of metaphors and similes. Then, create appropriate metaphors or similes to describe the characteristics of 10 different kinds of punctuation.	5 5 5 5 5 5 5 5 5

LAYER B

Week 15	Choose and complete one of the following activities	Points earned
Begin this assignment only AFTER you have completed and been tested on all chosen Layer C activities. This assignment will be evaluated according to a rubric which is attached to this syllabus. Due: 4/17	• Find any magazine article containing at least 10 paragraphs. Highlight all uses of punctuation. Be prepared to discuss the reasons for using the punctuation the writer did.	10
	• An activity for two people: Each choose an editorial essay from different issues of *TIME* or *Newsweek*. Be sure your partner does not know what you have chosen. Re-type the article **eliminating** all punctuation. Exchange papers and add the punctuation back into the essay. Then, "correct" each other's paper by highlighting any errors made.	10

LAYER A
THE CULMINATING ESSAY FOR THE COURSE

Week 16	Choose and complete one of the following activities	Points earned
Due: 4/23	• Analyze the text of Martin Luther King, Jr.'s "I Have a Dream" speech or his "Letter From a Birmingham Jail" essay (available on the Internet). Explain, in a well-written essay of at least 5 paragraphs, how his use of rhetorical strategies, stylistic techniques, and correct use of grammar and punctuation all contribute to making the speech or essay memorable and persuasive.	10
	• Analyze the text of any U.S. President's inaugural address. Explain, in a well-written essay of at least 5 paragraphs, how the use of rhetorical strategies, stylistic techniques, and correct use of grammar and punctuation all contribute to making the speech memorable and persuasive.	10

ASSESSMENT

The following descriptors (matched to points earned) are applicable to all the rubrics which follow:

5 = Exemplary
4 = Effective
3 = Acceptable
2 = Minimal
1 = Unacceptable (something was submitted, but cannot be evaluated based on the criteria),
0 = not submitted

EFFECTIVE STYLE RUBRIC
LAYER B

	5	4	3	2	1
Identifying examples	All appropriate examples are highlighted	Nearly all appropriate examples are highlighted	Many examples are highlighted, but a few wrong examples may be included	Some apt examples are highlighted, but many are not or may be wrong examples	The submission does not include highlighting of examples or may include only a few
Description	Includes precise definitions of coord/subord, a comprehensive accounting of the techniques used, and an insightful summary of the overall style	Includes definitions of coord/subord, an apt accounting of techniques used, and a summary of the overall style	Mentions coord/subord, accounts for some techniques used, but may not aptly summarize the overall style	May give a brief or cursory overview of techniques used, but may not summarize the overall style accurately	The submission does not describe coord/subord techniques or characterize overall style as the prompt asks
Writing style	Clear, concise, coherent description, with virtually no usage or surface errors	Clear, concise, coherent description, but may have a few usage and/or surface errors	Generally clear writing, but may have some redundancy in the description and several surface and/or usage errors	Somewhat clear writing, but the number of usage and surface and/or usage errors interferes with comprehension	The submission is incoherent

Scoring: Add up points earned _____ divide by 3 _____ × 2 = _____ Final Score

LAYER A

	5	4	3	2	1
Description	Includes comparison/contrasts that are insightful, from credible sources asked for, and precisely summarizes the overall style of the writers	Includes comp/contrasts that are apt, from the sources asked for, and summarizes the overall style of the writers	Includes comp/contrasts, from sources asked for, but may not fully summarize the overall style of the writers	May include comp/contrasts, but may not include all of the sources asked for and may not summarize the overall style of the writers well	The submission does not address the prompt
Writing style	Clear, concise, coherent description, with virtually no usage or surface errors	Clear, concise, coherent description, but may have a few usage and/or surface errors	Generally clear writing, but may have some redundancy in the description and several surface and/or usage errors	Somewhat clear writing, but the number of usage and surface and/or usage errors interferes with comprehension	The submission is incoherent

Scoring: Add up points earned _____ = _____ Final score

RHETORIC/ARGUMENT RUBRIC
LAYERS B AND A

	5	4	3	2	1
Use of rhetorical devices	Uses logos, pathos, ethos (*l*, *p*, & *e*) insightfully and skillfully throughout without using logical fallacies; makes a compelling argument	Uses *l*, *p*, & *e* throughout the argument with minimal use of logical fallacies; makes a good argument	Uses *l*, *p*, & *e* but may favor one element too much and/or may use a number of logical fallacies; makes an argument	Uses some *l*, *p*, & *e* but may overuse logical fallacies; the argument may include contradictions or otherwise be weak	The submission lacks *l*, *p*, & *e* appeals and/or overuses logical fallacies; may not present an argument at all
Claim and warrants	Thoughtful claim with a variety of insightful warrants to support the argument	Thoughtful claim with a variety of warrants	Makes a claim and uses some warrants	A claim may be vaguely evident, but may not be appropriate or fully supported	The submission does not include a claim at all or may have an inappropriate one or may not address the prompt
Writing/ Presentation style	Clear, concise, coherent with a positive, supportive tone	Clear, coherent with a positive tone	Is generally clear and coherent with a positive tone	May have some problems with clarity and coherence and/ or may have an inappropriate tone	The submission may lack clarity and coherence and/or have an inappropriate tone
Correctness	Clearly displays facility with language, syntax, and usage with virtually no mechanical errors	Displays facility with language, syntax, and usage, but may have a few surface errors	Displays some facility with language, syntax, and usage, but may have several surface errors	May have problems with language, syntax, and usage and/or numerous surface errors which interfere with comprehension	Has severe problems with language, syntax, and/ or usage which render the writing incoherent

Scoring:
Rhetorical devices points earned _____ × 4 = _____ +
Claim/warrants points earned _____ × 2 = _____ +
Style points earned _____ × 2 = _____ +
Correctness points earned _____ × 2 = _____ Total score

DOCUMENTATION RUBRIC
LAYERS B AND A

	5	4	3	2	1
Research	Thorough, using the highly appropriate sources asked for	Uses the appropriate sources asked for	Uses mostly appropriate sources most of the time	Uses sources, but they may not be as many as asked for or may not all be appropriate	Uses inappropriate sources or none at all
Argument	Includes an insightful claim, a variety of highly apt and compelling warrants & appeals; includes a thoughtful and thorough summary	Includes a claim, a variety of warrants & appeals; includes a thoughtful summary	Includes a claim and a few warrants & appeals; includes a summary	A claim may be vaguely evident, but may not be fully appropriate or may lack apt appeals and/or a summary	Is missing 1 or more key elements: claim, warrants, appeals, summary
Writing style	Clear, concise, coherent with a positive, supportive tone	Clear, coherent with a positive tone	Is generally clear and coherent with a positive tone	May have some problems with clarity and coherence and/or may have an inappropriate tone	The submission may lack clarity and coherence and/or have an inappropriate tone
Correctness	Clearly displays facility with language, syntax, and usage with virtually no mechanical errors	Displays facility with language, syntax, and usage, but may have a few surface errors	Displays some facility with language, syntax, and usage, but may have several surface errors	May have problems with language, syntax, and usage and/or numerous surface errors which interfere with comprehension	Has severe problems with language, syntax, and/or usage which render the writing incoherent

Scoring: Add up points earned _____ × 4 = _____ Final score

USAGE, PUNCTUATION, CORRECTNESS RUBRIC
LAYER B

	5	4	3	2	1
Requirements	Completes all requirements of the prompt thoughtfully and insightfully	Completes all requirements of the prompt thoroughly	Completes requirements, but may have a few minor omissions	May not complete all requirements and/or has more than a few omissions	The submission does not answer the prompt

Scoring: Add up points earned _____ × 2 = _____ Final score

LAYER A—CULMINATING ESSAY

(Same rubric as Unit 3, Layers B & A)

Scoring: Add up points earned _____ × 2 = _____ Final score

SUMMARY

In Chapter 6: *Convince Me- A Syllabus for a Freshman Composition Course Focused on Argumentative Writing*, a model was provided for developing a syllabus which focuses on content necessary for the effective writer of argument. Each sub-unit—(a) Effective Style; (b) Rhetoric/Argument; (c) Documentation; and (d) Usage/Punctuation/ Correctness—used the layered curriculum, a variety of engaging activities, and varied assessments. It was very process-oriented since it is about writing. The unit demonstrates that choice can lead to greater ownership of the writing process and, ultimately, to more confident and competent writers.

SELECTED BIBLIOGRAPHY

Axelrod, R. B. and Cooper, C. R. *The Concise Guide to Writing.* New York: St. Martin's Press, 1993.

Burling, Robbins. *English in Black and White.* Chicago: Holt, Rinehart, and Winston, 1973.

Elbow, Peter. *Writing with Power.* New York: Oxford University Press, 1981.

Elbow, Peter. *Writing without Teachers.* New York: Oxford University Press, 1973.

Flesch, Rudolf. *How to Write, Speak, and Think More Effectively.* New York: New American Library, 1960.

Goldberg, Natalie. *Writing Down the Bones: Freeing the Writer Within.* Boston: Shambhala, 1986.

Hairston, Maxine C. *Succesful Writing* (2nd ed.). New York: W.W. Norton, 1986.

Hickey, Dona J. *Developing a Written Voice.* Mountain View, CA: Mayfield Publishing Company, 1993.

Kolln, Martha. *Rhetorical Grammar: Grammatical Choices, Rhetorical Effects.* NY: Macmillan , 1991.

Kovacs, Edna. *Writing Across Cultures: A Handbook on Writing Poetry and Lyrical Prose.* Hillsboro, Oregon: Blue Heron, 1994.

Lamott, Anne. *Bird by Bird: Some Instructions on Writing and Life.* New York: Anchor Books, 1994.

Lanham, Richard A. *Revising Prose* (3rd ed.). New York: Macmillan, 1991.

Macrorie, Ken. *Telling Writing.* New York: Hayden Book Co., 1976.

Maimon, Elaine P., et al. *Writing in the Arts and Sciences.* Cambridge, MA: Winthrop, 1981.

Murray, Donald M. *The Craft of Revision.* Chicago: Holt, Rinehart, and Winston, 1991.

Murray, Donald M. *A Writer Teaches Writing.* Chicago, IL: Holt, Rinehart, and Winston, 1981.

Nunley, K. F. (2004). *Layered curriculum: The practical solution for teachers with more than one student in their classroom* (2nd ed.). Kearney, NE: Morris.

Shaughnessy, Mina. *Errors and Expectations.* New York: Oxford University Press, 1977.

Strunk, William Jr. and E.B. White. *The Elements of Style.* 3rd ed. New York: Macmillan, 1979.

Tate, M. (2003). *Worksheets don't grow dendrites: 20 instructional strategies that engage the brain.* Thousand Oaks, CA: Corwin Press.

Tate, M. (2004). *"Sit and get" won't grow dendrites: Professional learning strategies that engage the adult brain.* Thousand Oaks, CA: Corwin Press.

Williams, Joseph M. *Lessons in Clarity and Grace.* 3rd ed. New York: Harper Collins, 1989.

Zinsser, William. *On Writing Well.* 4th ed. New York: Harper Collins, 1990.

Zinsser, William. *Writing to Learn.* New York: Perennial, 1989.

ABOUT THE AUTHORS

Sharon L. Spencer earned her BA (1979) in Early Childhood Education from Guilford College, completed her M.Ed. (1982) in Elementary Education with a focus on Literacy at University of North Carolina, Greensboro, and her Ph.D. in Curriculum Instruction (1991) at the University of North Carolina, Chapel Hill. She is a professor in the Department of Curriculum, Instruction, and Professional Studies in the School of Education at North Carolina Central University, where she also serves as Assistant Dean and Director of Teacher Education. She is licensed in elementary, reading, academically and intellectually gifted, curriculum and instruction, and mentoring. She has received a teaching excellence award. Her writing focuses on mentoring and induction, as well as pedagogy across the curriculum. While literacy was her first love, mathematical literacy has also taken a strong hold on her heart. She has co-conducted Algebra Project teacher trainings in the southeast.

Sandra A. Vavra earned her BA (1971) in English from SUNY, Binghamton, and completed her graduate work in Curriculum and Instruction, earning an MAT (1993) and a Ph.D. (1995) at the University of North Carolina, Chapel Hill. She is a professor in the Department of English and Mass Communication at North Carolina Central University, where she directs the English Education Program. She has received several UNC-system awards for teaching excellence. Her current and past writing involves an examination of the connections between culture, communication/rhetoric, and pedagogy and the way the interplay among them affects literacy and learning. A collection she co-edited, *Closing the Gap: English Educators Address the Tensions between Teacher Preparation and Teaching Writing in Secondary Schools* was published in 2007. Her next project will focus on teaching 21st century writers.

INDEX

A

Accountability, 9
Adolescence (young adults), 13, 25, 45, 97, 98, 99, 100, 101, 102, 104, 105, 106, 108, 109, 113, 114
Achievement (student), x, 5, 7, 11, 12, 18
Advocacy (teacher on behalf of students), 5, 9
African American (Black, males, leaders), 2, 72, 81
Assessment (grading, strategies), 2, 3, 5, 6, 8, 9, 11, 16, 17, 73, 74, 100, 101, 103, 110, 120, 123
Authentic experiences (learning situations, real world tasks, grading practices), xi, 7, 9, 12, 15, 122
Autobiography (to promote learning communities), x

B

Best teaching practices (defensible, research-based), 4, 6, 7, 8, 10, 11, 12, 13, 16, 17, 18, 19
Bibliotherapy, xi
Biopoem, 29, 30, 31
"Brain-friendly" (teaching strategies, research), ix, xi, 7, 11, 12, 13, 14, 16, 17, 18, 19, 27, 47, 48, 55, 72, 75, 99, 120, 122, 123

C

Choice (student), 4, 7, 8, 10, 14, 15, 16, 26, 27, 28, 29, 43, 45, 46, 47, 48, 55, 98, 113, 122, 123, 125, 129, 130, 131, 132, 133, 134, 135, 136
Classroom management (practices, problems, ethical), 7, 9, 11, 15, 16, 17, 74, 101, 122
Collaborative/Cooperative learning (instruction in groups and pairs, team-building, class-building), 5, 6, 9, 10, 16, 18, 27, 47, 66, 72, 80, 81, 99, 106
Culture (community, global, international, trends) 71, 72, 73, 74, 75, 76, 77, 78, 79, 80, 81, 86, 93, 100, 101, 102, 106
Culturally responsive teaching (multicultural pedagogy), ix, 7, 8, 9, 11, 16, 17, 27, 47, 48, 55, 72, 73, 74, 100, 101, 120, 122, 123
Critical literacy, ix, x, xi, xii

The Perfect Norm, pages 145–148
Copyright © 2009 by Information Age Publishing

D

Dendrites, 12, 14
Differentiated instruction, 5, 6, 7, 8, 9, 11, 14, 15, 16, 17, 18, 19, 47, 59, 73, 74, 75, 100, 101, 113, 120, 122, 123
Direct instruction, 9
Disabilities (students labeled as), 2, 3, 4, 8

E

Engaging teaching practices, 4
Essential knowledge, 4, 6
ESL, 8

F

Fairness in grading, 8
Fish! Philosophy, 46, 48, 50, 51, 53, 55, 58, 59, 61, 62, 64, 66, 69
Flat (Friedman's concept, "world is flat") 72, 78, 118
Foldables©, 32, 50, 60, 61, 64, 66, 76, 80, 81, 83, 87, 98, 99, 106, 131, 134, 135
Framework for 21st Century Learning, 118
Future-ready skills, 118, 119

G

Gardner's multiple intelligences, 12, 13, 16, 18, 19
Gifted (education, students), 7, 10, 11
Grades (grading practices, distorted & authentic), 2, 3, 7, 15
Graphic organizers (matrices, K-W-L charts, mind maps), 11, 30, 39, 41, 44, 48, 49, 54, 75, 76, 77, 79, 81, 82, 87, 91, 98, 99, 101, 105, 106
Graphic novel, 25, 26, 38, 39, 43

H

High-achieving learners (gifted, talented), 6, 7
High-stakes testing (state, standardized, mandated, normative), 4, 7
Humor (affect on memory, classroom environment), xi, 12, 13, 15, 18
Hypothalmus-driven behavior, 13

I

ICT literacy (communications and technological literacy), 118
Identity, 26
Instructional shortsightedness, 4, 5

J

Journals (reading logs), 33, 49, 50, 55, 59, 125, 129, 131, 133

L

Layered curriculum©, 11, 13, 14, 28, 29, 44, 49, 50, 68, 75, 76, 98, 99, 100, 103, 104, 105, 106, 107, 108, 109, 110, 111, 112, 113, 122, 123, 141
Learning styles (preferences), 4, 5, 9, 113
Literacy (communication, skills), 3, 4, 9, 11, 26, 73, 75, 93, 120
Love languages, xi
Lyric circles (also Literature Circles), 28, 29, 36, 37, 41, 46, 47, 48, 49, 50, 55, 59, 64, 66, 68, 98, 99, 103

M

Marzano's nine essential teaching strategies, 12, 13, 18, 19, 47, 48,

50, 52, 53, 54, 55, 58, 59, 61, 62, 64, 65, 66, 67

Mastery (over subject matter, grading, rubrics), 123, 125, 128, 129, 136–141

Maus I and *II* (Art Spiegelman), 28, 29, 38, 39

McRel study, 47

Memory (in learning), 7

Mind styles, 5

Multicultural (culminating event, literature, pedagogy, statistics), 5, 6, 9, 10, 73, 80, 90, 100, 101

Multilevel instruction, 8

Multiple intelligences, 5

N

NC professional teaching standards (vision statement), 118, 119

NCTE/IRA, 27

Neural pathways, 13

Neuroscience (educationally focused, brain-based research), 7, 11, 14, 16, 17

No Child Left Behind (NCLB, engendering fear, humiliation), 3, 4, 8, 119

Number of minority students, 5, 6, 9, 10

Number of minority teachers, 6, 9, 10

O

Organizational change theory, 4

P

Pacing guide, 9

Professional teaching standards/vision (21st century), 5, 118, 119

Punishment (negative learning environment), 8, 13, 14

R

Reading disabled, 3

REM sleep (hardwiring learning, cross-referencing), 13

Renzulli's Enrichment Triad model, 75

Reptilian brain (primitive), 13, 14

Retrieval cues (hooks to learning), 13

Rubrics (examples), 31, 32, 33, 40, 42, 43, 51, 54, 56, 57, 58, 60, 63, 64, 65, 67, 68, 69, 82, 83, 84, 85, 86, 91, 92, 111, 112, 113, 136, 137, 138, 139, 140, 141

S

Small Town (John Mellencamp), 28, 29, 37, 38

Social justice (equitable democratic systems, learning environments), x, xi, 11, 15

Special education, 7

Standards-based education, 3, 8

Standard course of study, 27

Standardized tests (state-mandated), 2, 4, 5, 9, 11

Stress (affect on learning), 13

Student choice (control, centered), 4, 7, 10, 11, 14, 18, 122, 123

T

Tapestry (Carole King), 28, 29, 31, 32, 33

Teacher-centered pedagogy, 11

Teacher education licensure standards, 5

Teaching to the test, 3

Tears of a Tiger (Sharon M. Draper), 46, 47, 48, 50, 52, 60, 69

Technology (in the classroom, uses of), 27, 28, 29, 43, 73, 75, 76, 79, 80, 81, 83, 86, 87, 88, 89, 93, 99, 102, 103, 104, 114, 126, 130, 131, 132, 134, 136

The Seven Habits of Highly Effective Teens (Sean Covey), 46, 47, 49, 50, 61, 62, 66, 69, 70

This I Believe essay, 28, 29, 40, 41, 42

Transition to differentiated instruction (tips to manage it), 14, 15

Twenty-first century (goals, skills, students, living, teacher), 9, 11, 71, 120

W

Who Am I?/I Am poems, 28, 29, 34, 35, 36

Who Moved the Cheese? (Spencer Johnson), 46, 47, 49, 50, 67, 69, 70

Writing scores, 3

V

Voice (student, writer's), xi, 26, 44

Z

Zeitgeist (educational), 9, 119

Printed in the United States
143054LV00001B/11/P

9 781607 520337